Places of Memory:
Whiteman's Schools and
Native American Communities

Sociocultural, Political, and Historical Studies in Education
Joel Spring, Editor

Places of Memory:
Whiteman's Schools and Native American Communities
Alan Peshkin

Political Agendas for Education:
From the Christian Coalition to the Green Party
Joel Spring

Non-Western Educational Traditions:
Alternative Approaches to Educational Thought and Practice
Timothy Reagan

The Cultural Transformation
of a Native American Family and Its Tribe 1763–1995
A Basket of Apples
Joel Spring

Emergent Themes?

Places of Memory:
Whiteman's Schools and Native American Communities

Alan Peshkin

LAWRENCE ERLBAUM ASSOCIATES, PUBLISHERS
1997   Mahwah, New Jersey   London

Lawrence Erlbaum Associates, Inc., Publishers
10 Industrial Avenue
Mahwah, New Jersey 07430

Cover art by Danny Silverman

Library of Congress Cataloging-in-Publication Data

Peshkin, Alan.
Places of memory : whiteman's schools and Native American communities / Alan Peshkin.
     p. cm.
   Includes bibliograpical references.
   ISBN 0-8058-2468-5 (cloth : alk. paper). — ISBN 0-8058-2469-3 (paper : alk. paper)
    1. Indians of North America—Education—New Mexico. 2. Hispanic Americans—Education—New Mexico. 3. Mexican Americans—Education—New Mexico. 4. Discrimination in education—New Mexico.
   I. Title.
   E97.65.N6P47   1997
   306.43'09789—dc21   97–5612
                           CIP

Printed in the United States of America
10 9 8 7 6 5 4 3 2 1

*This book
is dedicated to
Jesse Peshkin McConnell
and
Sarah Peshkin McConnell.
They are significant components
of my places and memory.*

Contents

She had not understood, till she came to a place where it was lacking, the extent to which her sense of the world had to do with the presence of those who had been there before, leaving signs of their passing and spaces still warm with breath—a threshold worn with the coming and going of feet, hedges between fields that went back a thousand years, and the names even further . . . .

—David Malouf (1993)

Preface

The origin of a research project is sometimes as strikingly clear as the double rainbows I have seen over New Mexico's Sangre de Cristo Mountains. While visiting New Mexico in 1989, I was struck by the opportunity the state presents to continue exploring the school-community relationship, as I have done since 1972 in rural, religious, and multiethnic sociocultural settings (Peshkin 1978, 1982, 1986, 1991). In New Mexico I could learn about the school-community relationship within four major culture groups. The first of these four is the Native American, or *Indian,* as I generally refer to them because this is the term they use. The particular Indians I worked with are from the Pueblo[1] tribe. The Pueblo young people I studied attended Indian High School, a nonpublic school. (This is a pseudonym, as are the names of the three schools that follow.) The second group is Hispano (see Dozier 1983:90–96), or Spanish-American, who live in highland villages of northern New Mexico and trace their origins to Spain, having come via Mexico to the New Mexican outpost of the Spanish empire centuries ago. The Hispano students attended Norteño High School, a public school. The third group is Mexican, their long history a record of conquest, settlement, and migration to New Mexico. New Mexico's Mexican-American citizens of many generations are joined by a continuing stream of newcomers. The Mexican students attended Havens High School. Official state documents often conflate and refer collectively to the Spanish and Mexican groups as *Hispanic.* The fourth group is Anglo,[2] the newest of New Mexico's major subgroups. They are white people, internal migrants, who arrived largely

---

[1]*Pueblo* can refer to the collectivity of people known as the Pueblo Indians; to one of the 19 reservation locales where each different New Mexican Pueblo tribal group lives, as one might say, "When my work is done this afternoon, I'm driving home to my Pueblo;" or to an individual member of one of the Pueblo tribes. The 19 Pueblo tribes are joined, on the one hand, by history, language, religion, and some joint cultural and educational enterprises, but they live apart and are differentiated, on the other, by distinctions of history, language, and religion. Clarifying these distinctions is beyond the scope of my book, but see, for example, the writings of Dozier (1970), Eggan (1950), Parsons (1939), and White (1935, 1942, and 1962).

[2]In his dictionary of New-Mexican Spanish, Rubén Cobos defines *Anglo* as referring "to any white European mixture, particularly an English-speaking white person" (1983:10).

from eastern and midwestern states. They are a culturally diverse group, as are the other three, and perceived by the others as members of the nation's dominant group, its mainstream. The Anglo students in my study attended Edgewood Academy, a nondenominational, nonpublic high school.[3]

As my coauthors in this project and I see it, naming a group is properly the choice of the group itself. Though all persons within the four groups would not agree, the designations noted here—*Indian, Hispano, Mexican-American,* and *Anglo*—are the most generally accepted terms that we identified after long-term fieldwork in each setting. In the southwest, white people, technically identifiable as European-Americans, are called "Anglos." In short, we take recourse to insider usage, not to technical accuracy, political correctness, or the designations preferred by people living elsewhere.

Of the four studies that developed from my chance stay in New Mexico, I organized the research in the Indian and Anglo high schools, Shelley Roberts of the University of Illinois undertook the Hispano school–community study, and Marleen Pugach of the University of Wisconsin at Milwaukee, the Mexican. Each of the resulting books centers on one of these four cultural settings. Each is intended to stand alone; all but the Anglo study focus on the dual-world identity of New Mexico's three non-Anglo ethnic groups. Indian, Hispano, and Mexican children grow up aware that their ethnicity sets them apart from the dominant Anglo culture. At the same time, they unavoidably participate in the language and life of the larger American culture, itself far from unitary. In the dual-world challenges of New Mexican subcultures, we see aspects of our nation's conflicted focus on identity, that is, on the processes of cultural remaining and becoming as they play out in the lives of our native people and of our many voluntary and involuntary immigrant groups.

In the Anglo-majority school I studied, a place of substantial opportunity by any measure, I see the dominant Anglo experience writ large. Its students have access to the best that privileges Anglo society and that differentiates their experiences and opportunities from those of the other subgroups. Thus, the Anglo school is an exaggerated reflection of the so-called American main-

---

[3]All four schools we studied satisfied our major criterion—the ethnic group of interest was numerically dominant there. Beyond this, we needed schools that would willingly admit us and that did not present any unduly complicating factors (e.g., a brand new, inexperienced superintendent or principal) or a long-standing political controversy. We do not assume that Havens High is representative of other Mexican-American schools or that I could best learn about Native Americans only at Indian High School. We sought advice, depended on the invitations of well-wishers, and accepted access where it was offered and, on other grounds, seemed to make sense. We did hope to learn from the people in each school and community about a phenomenon that was of consequence to them, but also, in one way or another, of consequence to people and communities in many other settings, as well.

stream[4] and the counterpoint to the three ethnic-oriented schools and communities. Together the four studies form a portrait of schooling in New Mexico, perhaps similar to that in many other places as well. More generally, for my purposes they further document the range of ways that host communities in our educationally decentralized society use the prerogatives of local control to "create" schools that fit local cultural inclinations.

I think of the Indian, Hispano, Mexican, and Anglo studies as explorations of the interactions between cultural *remaining*,[5] as reflected in the students' traditions of home and community, and cultural *becoming*, as encouraged by the students' experiences in schools that historically have been established as agents of Anglo-American society. At best, there may be some tension in the generational differences between what children anywhere learn at school, and what their parents know and value. Such differences may embody disputed orientations between young and old about the substance of remaining and becoming. At worst, strain, confusion, and ambiguity may be generated by home–school and community–society orientations that are separated by a vast cultural divide. Pueblo Indian children and adults may feel the tension and strain of each case.

My study of the Pueblo Indians and Indian High School, the first of the project's four books, brought me once more to cultural terra incognita and another opportunity to be learner-as-researcher. Indian High School is a non-public, state-accredited, off-reservation boarding school for more than 400 Indian students, a large majority of them from Pueblo tribes, others from Navajo and Apache tribes. It operates under the joint auspices of New Mexico's 19 Pueblo tribes, whose governors appoint the school board members, and the federal government's Bureau of Indian Affairs, which both funds and has

[4]For further discussion of the meaning of the term *mainstream,* see Heath (1983:391–392). No term does full justice to the worlds beyond the ethnic subcultures of New Mexico or anywhere else. I would be hard put to add precision to a simple designation such as *mainstream* or *Anglo society* or *predominant culture.* What seems clear is that outside the ethnic subcultures are people, agencies, and institutions not only with pervasive economic and political power, but also with the populousness sufficient to establish norms and the power to impose them on others.

[5]Vanderbilt University professor Howard L. Harrod uses the concepts of *remaining* and *becoming* in *Becoming and Remaining a People: Native American Religions on the Northern Plains* (1995). His book's title captures the importance of these concepts for Harrod. In regard to contemporary Indian concerns for remaining, see Bruner (1986) and his discussion of the narrative shifts of studies of "Native American culture" from "the present as disorganization, the past as glorious, and the future as assimilation" to "the present as a resistance movement, the past as exploitation, and the future as ethnic resurgence" (139). Bruner's conception generally fits my personal experience and narrative focus. One major exception to Bruner's conception that I draw from my interviewing of Pueblo persons is that they continue to see a glorious, pre-Columbian, golden-age past.

property rights to the school, but acknowledges Pueblo rights to local control and self-determination. Pueblo control, managed through its school board, extends to the appointment of the superintendent and all academic and non-academic personnel. As a state-accredited school, Indian High School subscribes to curricular, safety, and other requirements of New Mexico. As a nonpublic school devoted to Indian students, it has the prerogative to be as distinctive as the ethnic group it serves.

Recalling well the tribal experience of past decades with non-Indian researchers, the Pueblo gatekeepers of my access to Indian High School were hesitant about my project. The permission they eventually gave me to study their school was couched in guarded language. This reflected both past disappointments with other researchers and some uncertainty about who I would prove to be and what I would write. But it was also couched in guarded expectation. A Pueblo leader conveyed the latter sense as we concluded our final interview session:

> I hope that this work you're doing is going to be successful, that you're going to be able to share with the non-Indian world, and that they do get something out of it. I know there's a lot of work out there that I look through and say to myself, "People don't need to read some of this stuff non-Indians have written." Maybe from what you write people will have a better understanding of where we're coming from, who we are, and accept us the way we are. That's the reason we allowed you this opportunity, because if we didn't feel comfortable with you, then I don't think we would have allowed you to be here. It's not easy for just any Tom, Dick, or Harry to come here.

I'm pleased not to have been taken "for just any Tom, Dick, or Harry," honored to have been permitted to undertake this research, and uneasy about the expectation to write for both a non-Indian audience, as charged by the Pueblo leader, and an Indian audience, as I think I ought to. Communicating to a non-Indian audience "a better understanding of where we're coming from" strikes me as an appropriate undertaking. Communicating to an Indian audience what I have learned strikes me as an appropriate responsibility.

ACKNOWLEDGMENTS

In the course of conducting and completing a study, I accumulate debts in many quarters: To those in school and community, the educators, students, and parents who open doors, hearts, and minds to let me learn; to those at home and university, my family, friends, and colleagues who inspire, support, and sustain my work in myriad ways; and to those at one's publishers, the editors and reviewers of Lawrence Erlbaum Associates, who bring insight and expertise to the complex task of creating a book. How indebted I am, and how grateful I feel! Indebtedness and gratitude extend most particularly to the Spencer Foundation for generous funding and yet one more vote of confidence; to the University of Illinois at Urbana–Champaign; and, not least, to the Center for Advanced Study in the Behavioral Sciences, where I completed prepublication revisions and benefitted from its extraordinary work ambience and provision of word processing, editing, critique, and overall support. Finally, I gladly express warmest thanks and appreciation to Mike Milstein, Kay Tenorio, Bonnie Page, and Ignacio Cordoba, all four associated with the University of New Mexico, whose advice, introductions, and support were essential in the critical matters of doing research in New Mexico, finding schools to study, and gaining access to them.

Long before I wrote this book's final chapter, I realized that I have never ceased to be impressed and influenced by Cheikh Hamidou Kane's remarkable novel, *Ambiguous Adventure* (1972), a story of remaining and becoming set in Islamic West Africa. It belongs in the special class of fiction writing that substantiates that some of the best, most faithful rendering of human affairs comes from gifted novelists, the models for many of us who think of ourselves as social scientists. A problem facing Pueblo people and many other Americans, as well, is that for them schools are an ambiguous adventure.

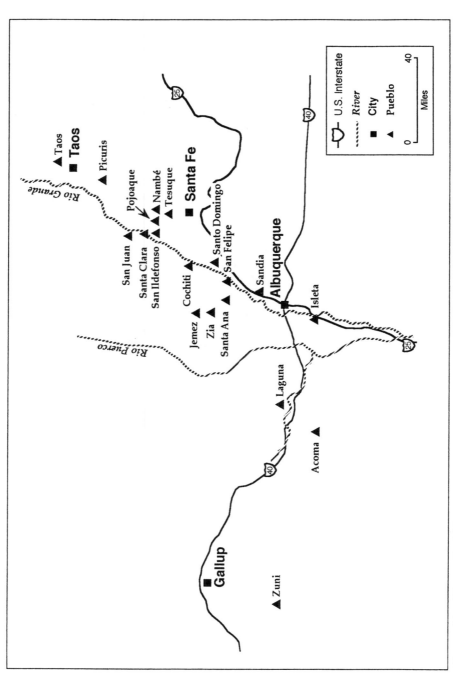

Created by Nancy Peshkin.

Prologue

Indians are American people whose tribal lives are point and counterpoint to the lives of other American people at community, state, and national levels. By claiming and reclaiming land, water, fishing, funereal, political, and religious rights, they are perceived to threaten events and decisions made at all three levels, and they in turn feel threatened by them. In fact, they prefer not to be victims or be seen as victimizing, as they exhort and claim and develop and litigate, as their needs require. Indians are increasingly deemed newsworthy in this day of multiculturalism, diversity, and renewed ethnic assertiveness.

A recent meeting to honor the oral tradition featured Simon Ortiz, a notable Acoma Indian poet, writer, and storyteller. The conference was called *Hama-Ha*,[1] words in Keres, a southern Pueblo language group, that mean, "A first dawn in the East, a time when all was one in the heart of the Creator" (Villani 1992:32). According to Ortiz, "Native American people base their lives on … three interrelated things: land, culture and community" (in Villani 1992:32). These are the essence of Pueblo Indian life and embrace their most profound concern for survival in traditional terms.

Pueblo people lost habitats to successive invaders who by conquest, squatting, and redefining how Pueblo land would be used were able to wrest it from Pueblo control (see Spicer 1962). In 1540, before the Spanish had a permanent colony in the area of modern-day New Mexico, there were an estimated fifty-three Pueblo communities (the exact number is moot), compared with today's nineteen, so concern for physical survival is not farfetched. The basis of this concern is evident in the fateful loss of another Indian tribe, the Chippewa.

> A treaty signed in 1867 set aside 837,000 acres of land for the White Earth Band of Chippewa. Today, Indians own less than 7 percent of the reservation, about

---

[1] Another source defines it as "listening and telling of stories" (Indyke 1994:18).

200 miles northwest of Minneapolis.... "The legal system has not worked well on our behalf," a Chippewa leader explained. "If we have to buy back our land, then that's what we have to do. Piece by piece. Inch by inch." [*New Mexican* 1992: A6]

In fact, among Indians loss is theme, source of despair, and rallying cry. The objects of loss include:

land—as noted above;

water—"Pueblo leaders say water settlements may be acceptable" (*New Mexican* 1992: A4)

language—"Indians Work to Save a Language—and Their Heritage" (*Education Week* 1992:1);

religion—"The 'Native American Free Exercise of Religion Act of 1993' was introduced ... to ensure religious freedom to Native Americans" (Kress 1993:5);

tradition—"Last week, over 200 people came ... to create the first all-Indian national organization dedicated to ... offering guidance on how to preserve and revitalize Indian traditions.... They call themselves, appropriately, 'Keepers of the Treasures'" (Aldrich 1991:6);

the *integrity of self*—Cherokee Chief Wilma ManKiller criticized the University of Illinois mascot, Chief Illiniwek: "I've met many progressive, intelligent people today, and yet what the outside world knows about this university is that you have a racist symbol" Oehlsen 1992:3);

and *the integrity of environment*—"Lena Bravo, a Hualapai elder in Arizona ... says her tribe's 1991 defeat of a uranium strip-mine ... depended more on the Great Spirit than on legal maneuverings.... 'We realized this was a question of tearing up our Mother Earth'" (Knox 1993:54).

These objects of loss are integral to tribal survival. Responses to these losses are collective matters between tribes and their neighbors, and between tribes and state and federal governments.

Disconcerted by the images of his people often held by non-Indians, Mateo Romero, a young Pueblo painter and Dartmouth College graduate, tried to set the record straight: "People think of Native American Indians in these noble, savage stereotypes. In reality, they're just human beings like everybody else" ("New Traditions from New Mexico" 1991:12). Being "like everybody else," however, is belied by the reality of lives shaped by these many objects of loss, but also by the recurrent mention by Pueblos of their dual-world existence and the resulting complications.

In 1990, for example, Pueblo mother Bonnie Candelaria[2] enrolled her daughter in a public school located outside San Felipe reservation, where she lived (Barringer 1990:B9). Tribal authorities protested her decision to remove her child from the local reservation school and, thereby, from the influence of her tribe. Candelaria argued for her child's need "to learn to adapt to the world out there, rather than the world in here." It is debatable whether tribal authority, established under the circumstances of tribal sovereignty[3] as a nation-within-the-nation, extends to parental decisions about where reservation members send their children to school. That tribal authorities can even consider it a possibility indicates the magnitude of the issue of if and how children are to be socialized for Indian culture and community. Sam Montoya, Pueblo Indian and Bureau of Indian Affairs official, placed this issue in the perspective of the dual-world challenges and opportunities that confront his people:

> Some people are waking up and saying we have to be more aggressive about protecting our way of life. We have existed here for hundreds of years ... There is an awareness now that, yes, there is a challenge to these values. I'm not trying to say that any tribe is trying to shut out the outside world. They're trying to strike a balance between what they feel is unique ... and the new opportunities provided by the other world. [quoted in Barringer 1990:B9]

Many Americans have grown up informed by and living to varying extents in two worlds. As generations pass, the distinctiveness of their subgroup culture diminishes, sometimes to the vanishing point. Indian cultures are decidedly different. In no other American group is there a Sam Montoya who can speak as he did after 500 years of culture contact between Indians and non-Indians.

---

[2]In this chapter and elsewhere, where I make reference to persons cited in newspapers, magazines, and the like, I do not use pseudonyms. There is no need. Otherwise, when I refer to persons I observed at work or interviewed, I use pseudonyms, in keeping with the commitment I made.

[3]Reference to "Indian nations" may have the ring of overstatement, bombast, and farce, but it is none of this to Indian leaders who simultaneously depend on federal funding for survival, acknowledge the laws and power of the non-Indian world, and persist in claiming sovereignty in terms comparable to those of other nations: a status that cannot be bestowed and cannot be taken away, but that inheres in one's peoplehood. One day a Pueblo governor spoke these words to an Indian High School civics class: "Governor King [then New Mexico's governor] is open to negotiate with us on a good basis, but the whole state of New Mexico does not recognize us. I had to give up some of my sovereignty just to get funding for a senior citizens program. You don't want to give up what belongs to you. The more programs we get funded, the more we give up. We need funding without strings."

For a discussion of sovereignty stimulated by the current issues of Indian casinos on reservation land see Vizenor (1994:138–48).

Or a puzzled Lena Bravo whose cultural upbringing has her wonder, "It's hard for us to even comprehend that there are different laws for religion, for the environment, and for the economy" (quoted in Knox 1993:84). In the governing structures of no other American group is there a hint of the sovereignty, with its assertions of autonomy, that laces discussions between Indian tribes and the several levels of government in "the other world"; nor does any other group relate to the federal government by treaty, and have its own federal bureau with its own bureaucracy.

Sovereignty extends to matters large and small. Take the case of Esther Nahgahnub, Chippewa Indian, who owns a .303 rifle, and sees sovereignty as applicable to matters relating to ceremony. She went hunting in search of a "bull moose to roast over a ceremonial fire." What Minnesota state officials called poaching, Ms. Nahgahnub called her rights. "'With me,' she said, 'sovereignty cuts through all the crap and says that I can take that moose for that ceremony'" ("Indians push Sovereignty Issue" 1993:1). A 1991 report of the Native American Rights Fund included a map of the United States with red dots placed in states where there was an ongoing issue arising from what Indian sovereignty possibly entails. No other American group could make a case for what underlies these red dots, which stretch across 20 states and embrace land claims, tribal recognition, jurisdiction, accountability, hunting rights, water rights, constitution development, restoration, reburial, religious freedom, and fishing rights (Lurie 1991:4).

II

An American institution: it is Friday night. Indian High School's basketball team is playing a home game. Students, usually long gone for the weekend to their reservation homes, spill out of the school's several male and female dormitory buildings. They merge with the procession of cars and pickup trucks heading toward parking lots next to the gym. The gym is packed. Students, teachers, parents, and relatives mill about in the gym lobby, greeting friends, buying food and drink, anxious to return to their seats before the national anthem is sung. Then the game begins.

I have watched high school teams play basketball since my own student days. Never before had I seen a team play like Indian High School's varsity squad. They were quick, athletic, and relatively short—shorter than their opponents, who came from a non-Indian school in their non-public school athletic league. The home team won the game, but it was how they played the game that fascinated me: a full-court press, their basic strategy, literally overwhelmed their opponents. Indian High School players swarmed at both ends of the court.

Sometimes I'd count the players on the floor, in disbelief that a legal five were able to do such damage. The result was one fine game in an overall winning season.

Many months later, I began my year-long contact with Indian High School and observed students at work in their classrooms. Regrettably, I saw no academic counterpart to this stellar athletic performance. Indian students take to and excel in the non-academic aspects of their school life. They acknowledge that they can and ought to achieve more academic success; they are disappointed that they do not.

About 1 month into my observations of Indian High School students in their classrooms, I decided that my initial fascination with the dual-world character[4] of the student's lives—the one, their traditional, tribal, Indian, reservation world, the other, the mainstream American, dominant Anglo, non-Indian world—would be oriented to exploring why these students reacted as they did in their classrooms.[5] From their school's many documents, I knew it had accepted as one of its main purposes helping students "to make fulfilling life choices." *Life choices* cover much ground. The choice of most interest to me—doing well in and with schooling—did not appear to be fulfilled.

In class, students generally were well-behaved and respectful. They were not rude, loud, or disruptive. More often they were indifferent. Their posture, their language, and their work displayed their disinclination to play the game of school the way their teachers daily invited them to play it. Hours of talk with teachers confirmed what I saw: teachers could not get students to work hard consistently, to turn in assignments, to participate in class, or to take seriously either the immediate (in-school) or the long-term (after-graduation) consequences of their classroom performance. Hours of talk with students confirmed what the teachers said: students were aware of what by their own standards is

---

[4]Nobody I spoke with in the Pueblo community ever elaborated what they knew and what I fully accept to be the case: they live in complex, multiple worlds. The two-world usage is their shorthand designation. It is drawn from their sense of an inside Indian world and an outside non-Indian world. By concentrating throughout this book on the dual identity of the students, I thereby understate other aspects of their lives. For my purposes, they were not just young men and women, adolescents, students, Indian youths, and the like. They were dual-world persons, a transfiguring that highlights their Pueblo *and* non-Pueblo dimensions of self and community. Thus, not seen in any fullness are: the students as students, portrayed in their daily round in classrooms, playing fields, dormitories, and elsewhere; the students as sons and daughters at home in the places that constitute ordinary Pueblo life; and the students as individuals who grow up, fall in love, raise a family, aspire to a good life, and hope for personal success and recognition. Given more possibilities for characterization than anyone can capitalize on, one inevitably selects and creates and shapes a narrative.

[5]As a result of this decision, my study assumed a more definite problem-driven focus than it would have otherwise.

their unsatisfactory classroom performance, they wished it were otherwise, and they knew why it should be otherwise. In the words of one student: "The basis for learning what we do learn is because we have to function in the working world, in a white-dominated society.[6] Life wouldn't be very rewarding if you don't have a job. You can't get a car, a house, a lot of things you need just for basic living." And in the words of another:

> Well, the jobs now, you need a higher education. So, if you really want to have money and raise a family, and stuff, you have to have a good job.... I just want to go out and see the world. I don't really want to stay home [like her sister, who had one child, broke up with her boyfriend, found herself a new boyfriend, and had a second child]. I want to go and do something, and then come back [to her reservation].

Several circumstances frame these students' comments. The sister referred to here is like numerous other young women in families throughout the tribes who begin high school with a promising display of intelligence, interest, and academic success that evaporates before high school is formally over; other women show academic promise by solid success in high school that stops short before the first year of college is formally over. Perhaps as many as 75% of all Indian students nationwide leave their colleges and universities before they have completed the first year. Moreover, they have the lowest ACT scores and the highest high school dropout rates of all ethnic groups in New Mexico.[7] Indian High School's exceptionally low dropout rate is an anomaly that is achieved, I infer from its own statistics, by the high transfer-out rates, mostly in the ninth grade, which leads students back home to their local public high schools. Life at a boarding school is not to everyone's taste.

On the reservations from which the students come, per capita income is well below the national average, and unemployment rates among persons of working age at the different reservations is punishingly high. Students often invoked an image of groups of out-of-school young men at home idly standing around; comparably situated young women take care of babies.

The students' school, Indian High School, is administered and controlled by Indians who are dedicated to creating an environment congenial to its Indian students. Moreover, the school possesses resources, such as number of teachers,

---

[6]This student recognizes what others have pointed out as the involuntary acculturative act of needing to "learn the new culture to survive economically" (cited in LaFromboise, Coleman, and Gerton 1993:397).

[7]For documentation of poor academic achievement among Indians in the past, see Wax, Wax, and Dumont (1964).

library holdings, and computers, and enhancements from successful grant writing, sufficient to create opportunities better than all but the most favored schools in the entire state of New Mexico. The mission of the school is affirmed by Pueblo leaders in statements such as these:

> I feel it is important to emphasize to them [students] that nowadays [tradition] is not enough because our world has got so complex. The survival just for monies to eat, to have a home ... it's great to have the spirituality and the belief and the faith in your own ways, which we do have, but it's also necessary to feed yourself and not depend on welfare. I feel education is the biggest necessity to survive in the non-Indian world.

Meanwhile other leaders, in this case a teacher at Indian High School, are pointing out: "But to be successful in both [worlds] ... it's like a catch-22, where, you know, along the way you're compromising your own values, but in the long run you're trying to save those same values for the whole community."

In the year of my study at Indian High School, the superintendent arranged for an inquiry among reservation adults, and among the school's staff, students, and teachers, that would create a data base for their own long-range planning. In quiet, understated language, containing no hint of crisis or alarm, the report of this inquiry included three statements of needs: "a need to build and improve student self-esteem in order to enhance the chance of student success," "a need to improve student motivation in order to enhance the chance of student success," and "a need to improve student attitudes toward education, classroom behavior, homework and teachers/staff." The statement of this third need omits reference, as in the first two needs, to a relationship between student attitudes and their success.

This book examines why these three needs exist: why, in short, the relatively abundant resources, the good intentions of Indian High School educators, and the goals and aspirations of parents and students do not create "student success." In addition, the book addresses the matter of cultural duality. At home, Pueblo students learn to place their tribal communities at the center of their loyalty, affect, responsibility, and support. But they attend a school whose origins and rationale are in non-Indian society. It is a school designed for becoming effective in mainstream America, which effectiveness Pueblo students and their parents accept as requisite for their economic well-being, Thereby hangs my tale of the whiteman's school and the Native American community, of living in two worlds, of cultural survival.

1

The Focus of Memory: School and Community

It is hard to live our lives in places where we have no memories. It limits the depth of our relationships—not just to people, but to places, to seasons.

—*Kathleen Stocking, 1990*

PLACES OF MEMORY

Unremarkably, memory reverberates in our lives. We fear its loss, mark its diminishing as a frightening sign that the end of meaningful life is near, and marvel at those who remember well and truly what has happened to themselves and others. We chide ourselves for forgetting events that spouses, children, and friends expect us to bear in mind and respond to in proper ways. Our memory is the great tracker of what has gone by and what is present; our memory inspires what is to come. Of course, memory also marks places with flavor, affect, and tone. Places, to be sure, don't have memory; they enshrine memory, or they do not. We connect memory to locales, so that certain places haunt or frighten us, while others inspire warm or uncomfortable feelings, recall security or unease.

Some years ago, I visited an elementary school in Illinois, formerly a high school when the village it served was larger and could support an entire K–12 school system. The occasion of my visit was also one for parents to come and inspect their children's work. To pass time between appointments, I browsed through the long ground-floor corridor whose walls contained rows of pictures—the graduating seniors of decades past. A man soon joined me, a dad and a former graduate. He, too, examined the photographs. His picture was up there in the lines of now-fading visual emblems of glorified adolescence. I gazed upward just with curiosity, looking at student family names as markers of national origin, at hair and clothing styles, at signs of maturity—somehow, past graduates always look older than those I know today, and, of course, older than I believe I did at the same age. I tried to figure out if the student identified as class president looked presidential—a foolish game, but, then, I was merely passing time.

Not so the onlooking dad at my side. When he reached his own class picture, he looked up long and intently. In fact, he looked with reverence, as if standing before a shrine composed of images of sacred youth. For him, his class graduation photograph symbolized what, projecting, I could think he remembered as his golden youth, a time of innocence and promise, a time of days filled with simplicity in his life, his community, and, indeed, his world. The memory he conjured up, I presumed, included a distant time in his life, but also a distant place, not the aging, dingy setting of his young child's education. Time and place conspired to transfix him. He looked transfixed, and I felt like an intruder with my superficial, time-passing ways. Lacking memory, I could but play at making something out of what his memory could invest with such reality and such merit as to bring him to worshipful posture.

More recently, I heard a woman being interviewed on National Public Radio. One part of her family lived in Miami, one part in Cuba, her family's native home. The interviewer probed for her comparative attachment to the United States and to Cuba, inviting her to explore her preferred sense of identity, and to disclose where she saw the promise of her future. The woman finally said, "I don't think I can ever be American. I'm Cuban. I can't leave." Cuba—her stronger place of memory—embraced not only where an important part of her past was situated, but also what was currently essential in her life: where her mother lived, where she worked, where her friends and neighbors were, and where who she was—in the language she spoke, the food she ate, the music she hummed, and all her ways of knowing—were natural. What she knew and who she knew herself to be were Cuban, and this required no explanation, no justification, no unease about its appropriateness. She was not pleased with all that it meant to be Cuban, let alone satisfied with the material conditions of her life, her mother's health, and the prospects of her country given its loss of the decades of Soviet economic and military aid. She need not be fond of all her memory encompassed to take what it afforded as the substance for identity, dignity, and meaning.

I cling to the notion of places of memory,[1] persuaded that in the differential quality and meaning of what Pueblo people have stored in individual and collective memory lies the best explanation of why they respond as they do to

---

[1]For a useful discussion of memory, see Harrod's reference to "communities of memory" (1995: xvii and 102).

two tangled processes: one, going to the whiteman's[2] school and seeking some place in the world where that school belongs; the other, growing up Indian within a tribal community encompassed by the non-Indian world. It is premature to elaborate the consequences of these two processes, but not what is at stake for Pueblo people. Although attendance is compulsory, Pueblo adults freely send their children to school. The school, a Pandora's box of uncertainties and prospects, welcomes the children, and in the name of education and opportunity unwittingly unleashes a flood of activities that changes their lives forever. Under prevailing circumstances, can any school that Indian children now attend, even one controlled by Pueblo Indians who are attuned to Pueblo ideals, manage the impact of this stream of activities in a way that creates less confounding results?

REMAINING AND BECOMING

The formative years of approximately 5 to 16 are a critical time for shaping children's identity and preparing them for adult life. Parents, accordingly, may seek just the right nonpublic or public school, hoping to find one that incorporates moral values, academic standards, peer companions, if not a way of life, that fits their personal sense of worthy cultural norms. Home schooling may be the extreme case of parents' locating the exactly right academic milieu formed in their own interests. For such parents, no external institution will do. Other parents, no less conscientious, find the right educational fit with their sense of cultural norms in the local public schools. For them, no alternative is necessary.

The many types of nonpublic and public schools may differ in truly substantial ways. For example, the academic experience in denominational schools may be framed by an embracing religious orientation (see Peshkin 1986). The academic experience in nondenominational schools includes distinctions derived from philosophy, as in Waldorf and Montessori schools, and from soaring aspiration, as in the elite prep schools of the Northeast and elsewhere. Although such schools satisfy the tastes and needs of some families, they are objectionable to others.

---

[2]*Whiteman*, used throughout the book most often as one word, follows its similar usage in A. Richard King's book, *The School at Mopass* (1967), and George Spindler's rationale, located in a footnote in that book's foreword. *Whiteman* refers to people in the dominant society and "is not pronounced as two words" (King 1967: vii). This usage follows most particularly from anthropologist Keith Basso's *Portraits of "the Whiteman"* (1979).

No school or philosophy of schooling satisfies everyone. For most parents, the ideal school sustains the valued cultural norms of home and community, and readies their child to function productively and profitably in society at large. Parents fear for their own and their children's well-being if their children become misfits in their community or social class, on the one hand, or the larger society, on the other. Parents may vilify, abandon, or try to change schools they perceive as leading their children astray or failing to satisfy expected standards. By one means or another, parents expect schools to do good, or at the very least to develop their child's means to perform usefully as workers and citizens; they expect, as well, the school not to do harm to the family's cultural norms. It is one thing if the school does not actively promote these norms; not all parents want schools to play this role. But it is another if the school subverts these norms in any way, be it by insensitivity, inadvertence, or intent.

Many American subgroups, some of them racial, ethnic, cultural, or religious minority groups, seek to sustain their sense of a distinctive way of life, while facing the prospects of schooling in the dominant society. Troubled by the perceived outcomes of such schooling, minority parents may seek educational alternatives in Afrocentric, Chicano-centric, or parochial schools. These parents are doing what many parents always have done: seeking the best possible match between their own cultural norms and their child's school.

In the late 1960s, writer Stan Steiner traversed the country to gather perspectives on what American Indians "think about American society, about their own cultures, about the future" (1968:292). While preparing to write *The New Indians,* he came across a poem by David Martin Nez, "New Way, Old Way" :

We shall learn all these devices the White Man has.
We shall handle his tools for ourselves.
We shall master his machinery, his inventions,
his skills, his medicine, his planning;
But we'll retain our beauty
And still be Indian. [Steiner 1968:131]

Steiner cites the reaction to this poem by an anonymous official of the Bureau of Indian Affairs:[3] "Romantic but unrealistic ... These Indians have got to leave their dreams back there on the reservations and get into the real world" (1968:131). Almost 30 years later, Dr. Perry G. Horse (Kiowa), echoes the conclusions of David Martin Nez: "We are mindful that we do not live in the past. We know we must balance the best of our ways with those of others in our contemporary lives" (Horse 1994:8).

---

[3]This is an office of the federal government that oversees Indian High School and all other matters of policy and finance that pertain to officially recognized Indian life throughout the United States.

Nez and Horse are concerned with Indian mastery in two worlds, neither to be forgone, intent that even after learning "all these devices the White Man has" they will "still be Indian." For them and their native compatriots, the economically, politically, and technologically dominant world of the whiteman is the world from which they draw the imperatives of who they must consider becoming. If this world is never very distant from Indian life, it is nonetheless the Indian's second world, the place to which they go when they leave home.

Constructed from the norms and work needs of American society, Indian High School is a centerpiece in the world of becoming. It embodies the whiteman's form and content of cognition, affect, and skills. Indian High students get peer reinforcement for elements of this world pertaining to dress, food, music, sports, and material goods. The routines and preferences of Indian High School students are like those of students anywhere in the country. Although they have adopted and adapted to Anglo-American ways, and thereby become participants in that world, they continue to retain Pueblo ways, particularly regarding Pueblo ideals of who to be and what to value. Indeed, they remain Indian, even as they become recognizably mainstream Americans. As I will make clear in the following chapters, like Nez and Horse, most Pueblo parents believe that while their children must become skillful actors in the dominant society, they should remain faithful members of their tribal community.

This book is most immediately about Pueblo adolescents and their life as students at Indian High School, but it is most fundamentally about remaining and becoming, processes of consequence that everyone experiences in some way, to some degree. Typically, the issue is not *if*, for example, we will remain adherents to the behavior and beliefs of our family, our community, and our tradition, but *to what extent*.

Issues of remaining and becoming are intrinsic in the human condition. They are defined and redefined by circumstances beyond our control—economic booms, revolutions, war, and natural disasters; by circumstances we create or want to happen—becoming a dancer, becoming rich, or becoming a religious convert; and by circumstances of our being—an immigrant, a member of a minority group, a refugee, or a conquered foe. The general issues of remaining and becoming exist for everyone, but differ for each person in their particulars, as is clear from this brief consideration of the range of circumstances that can define them. Furthermore, they are inescapable issues. We do not have the option of living exactly like our parents or grandparents, of learning just what they knew and valued, absorbing it, and transmitting it to our own children—as comfortable and appealing as this option may be. In fact, no one has this luxury. As we learn, we make decisions, and we have decisions thrust upon us, of what to blend and balance, of what to accept, of what to keep intact and modify, from the interacting circumstances we face in our worlds of remaining and becoming. Schools are places of controversy because they are at the juncture of the processes of remaining and becoming, where what is at stake for society, local communities, parents, and students becomes explicit.[4]

I will explore the processes of remaining and becoming as they affect the educational experiences of Pueblo Indian adolescents who live in their tribal reservation communities and attend Indian High School. I do not fully explore this school and its operations; this important topic is not the point of my inquiry. My consideration of remaining and becoming illuminates the matter of schooling anywhere these youngsters would attend school, which is to say that though I focus my study on Indian High School, I mean to affirm that there are basic circumstances about the whiteman's schools that generally make them problematic for Pueblo adults and children.

NATURE OF STUDY

Mimes perform a skit within a circle of light standing on an otherwise blackened stage. When a mime moves and "bumps" into the "walls" of this light, the audience realizes that the mime has fashioned light into a fully enclosing container. He moves this way and that in an effort to escape his imagined confines. With every bewildered move, he knocks against a barrier invisible to the audience, but nonetheless impassable. The mime apparently can see through his enclosure, but he cannot move beyond its constraints.

The circumstance of an unseen but effectively constraining barrier between the mime and the world outside the circle of light comes to mind when I consider the issue of academic success for Indian High School students. For the purposes of my study, I make several assumptions. First, the students—of high school age, living on or closely associated with their reservations, and members of one of the New Mexican Pueblo Indian tribes—have intellectual capacities comparable to any American group. Second, they are taught, for the most part, by talented, caring educators. And, third, they are raised by families that generally value education. Assumption number one is in the stands-to-reason category. Assumptions number two and three rest on the outcomes of my observations of several years, and also on the students' assessments reported in later chapters.

In light of these assumptions, I ask, as do Indian High School educators: What, then, is the barrier that stands between students and academic achieve-

---

[4]The struggle to shape educational purpose and practice involves many actors. Schools are embedded institutions; many agencies have a stake in their form and outcome (Peshkin 1995).

ment so they do less well than their peers in New Mexico; less well than their teachers want them to do and believe they can do; less well than their parents and communities want and need them to do; and less well than the students acknowledge they can and should do?[5] Doing "less well" is not a term explicitly defined by those within this Pueblo school and community who use it. It covers a range of conventional indications of "success": test scores, grade point averages, motivation and effort, graduation rates, college applications, persistence in college, and acquiring jobs based on school achievement.

The institutionally completed act—schooling offered by educators to students, schooling received and made use of by students[6]—is a complex, hit-and-miss affair. It requires the connection of educator intentions and deeds with student will and capacity to translate those intentions and deeds into practice.

---

[5]John Ogbu, Henry Trueba, Frederick Erickson, Hugh Mehan, Kathryn Au, Cathie Jordan, Roland Tharp, and other prominent scholars have explored the issue of the academic achievement of minority children in American schools, particularly those children from what Ogbu (1978, 1987) calls involuntary minority groups. The resulting literature informs us of explanatory factors relating to views of success, social class distinctions, cultural discontinuities, group ideologies, and the like. By no means do I minimize these contributions to understanding the phenomenon of school success, especially those of John Ogbu. They do apply to the school behavior of Indian children. In this study, I focus on one among the many possible explanatory factors—the cultural and political singularity of the Pueblo Indian community. For relevant general discussion on how minority students fare in school, see Jacob and Jordan's edited volume on *Minority Education* (1993) with its seminal papers by Erickson and Ogbu, but also by Moll, Diaz, Gibson, and many others, and the special issue of *Anthropology and Education Quarterly* (*18*(4): 1987). See also Foley's article and citations (1991), Trueba's commentary on Foley and his own citations (1991), Mehan, Hubbard, and Villanueva's fine paper (1994), and Suárez-Orozco's chapter (1990). For relevant particular discussion on Native Americans, see Fuchs and Havighurst (1972), Philips (1983), Dehyle (1991, 1992), and Reyhner (1992). For the most effective pedagogical reform efforts, see the work done at Kamehameha Schools in Honolulu (Jordan 1984 and 1985; Au 1980; Au and Jordan 1981; Tharp and Gallimore 1988). The question I do not ask is the one Wolcott clarified in his conclusions to *A Kwakiutl Village and School*. Though he began his study intending to explore "why Indian pupils fail in school," he shifted to a question he thought to be less narrowing: "How do the schools fail their Indian pupils?" (Wolcott 1967:131), which is a consideration of consequence to McDermott (1974, 1987) and McDermott and Gospodinoff (1979). In fact, I believe I do not ask either question. Most closely related to my representation here is Wax, Wax, and Dumont's study of schooling of Sioux children at Pine Ridge. Three related "theories" undergird their inquiry: "cultural disharmony," "lack of motive," and "preservation of identity" (1964:13 and passim). Their original theories make more sense to me than their conclusion that:

> it was the children who were successfully sabotaging the process of learning, not because they disliked learning, but as part of the development of their own group discipline. (Wax 1971:263)

[6]There is, of course, a world of meaning in the unelaborated verbs "offered" and "received," but I trust my basic intention is clear.

There is always a discrepancy between the fullness of what educators offer and the extent to which students can and will accept and capitalize on what they are offered. Ideally, students value their school's academic opportunities for their own sake and for their relevance to post-school opportunities. Between educators' ideals and students' behavior is the latter's understanding of their school experience. Indian High School students do not consistently grasp and internalize the prospects of schooling in ways that effectively motivate them to persist in learning.

By taking educators, parents, and students to be relatively inconsequential factors in creating this circumstance, I de-emphasize factors that elsewhere can and do make a difference for student achievement. I focus on the cultural barriers between students[7] and academic achievement, aware that by doing so I venture into territory that I cannot comprehensively explore because of the deep-rooted taboos within which Pueblo Indians place traditional cultural knowledge.

Barred as I was by my willing agreement with school authorities (superintendent and school board) from acquiring such knowledge, I am left to infer and imagine how to connect culture and schooling in ways that illuminate a thorny, exasperating problem. My conjecturing is based on contact with Indian High School over a 3-year period, including one stretch of 11 consecutive months, when I lived in an Indian High School house located on its 100-year-old campus of 34 buildings, dispersed over 100 acres. The campus is an Indian island of sorts set within the sprawl of one of New Mexico's moderate-sized cities. Beyond school boundaries are the sights and sounds of what students call "the real world."

During my 11 months' residence, I arranged extensive, multisession interviews with Pueblo and non-Pueblo teachers and counselors and with Pueblo students and staff. Of the nearly 100 persons I interviewed, approximately 85 were Pueblos. Participant observation took me to all formal and informal aspects of the school, where I was allowed unlimited access to all people and places. In addition, I was able to attend public ceremonial occasions at the various Pueblos and make informal visits to the reservation homes of friends and their relatives. I expect to discuss the school–culture connection without violating the taboos that I promised to respect as a condition of gaining access to conduct my research. Honoring this promise affects all that I did, beginning with my data collection and extending to the writing of this book.[8]

Accordingly, I, too, am like the mime within an enclosure of light. I am, moreover, committed to stay enclosed. Words alone were available to me to

---

[7]Unless otherwise stated, any reference to students or Indian students means the Pueblo Indian students who attend Indian High School and, when they are not at school, live at their reservations. Students from other tribes also attended the school.

[8]I am not the first person to honor such a commitment. Stan Steiner acknowledges that "There are many things the Indians did not wish told in this book.... Once again I have respected their wishes ... it was what we had agreed...." (1968:297).

grasp what my "enclosure" constrained me from apprehending directly in the conduct of Pueblo community life. Thus was I circumscribed in my inquiry. I do not chafe at this limit, whose grounding in the fundamentals of Pueblo life I accept without qualification. If at one time in my research life I wished I could unilaterally set the terms of my research, I no longer think this is beneficial from any perspective.

The words I elicited from Pueblo youth and adults were produced by questions that never asked about religion. My respondents could and did say, as they judged necessary, "I can't explain further," leaving unsaid what was redundant to add: to explain further would mean to touch on matters of religion, the foundation of Pueblo tribal communities. They not only unquestioningly accept the necessity of this taboo, they unerringly observe it in practice, thereby bespeaking an astonishingly high degree of consistency and coherence in Pueblo life, as well as effective socialization, notwithstanding a fair share of disrupting stresses and strains.

Strictly speaking, to discuss Pueblo life in almost any way is to enter the realm of religion; fortunately, the boundaries of secrecy do not embrace every expression of Pueblo life. Even the most traditional member of the most traditional Pueblo tribe will discuss to some extent defining attributes of Pueblo life, such as respect, community, participation, harmony, and the like. From within the degree of disclosure permitted by the limits of Pueblo secrecy I sought to learn about the constraints to academic success of Pueblo Indian adolescents.

This narrative builds on Vine Deloria Jr.'s idea of Indian association with Western civilization as "culture shock" (1991:250). Indian High School documents speak of "establishing balance between the two societies" and of "nurturing ... Indian values of respect, harmony, and hard work as a basis for making fulfilling life choices in an Indian and non-Indian world." By these intentions, Indian High School educators hope to help students escape the need to choose between either the world of shock or the world of comfort.

On the bulletin board of an Indian High School classroom, the teacher has pinned Shawnee Indian Tecumseh's famous words: "I am the maker of my own fortune, and Oh! that I could make that of my Red people, and of my country, as great as the conceptions of my mind."[9] The conceptions of Pueblo Indian minds are shaped by the instructions of the *kiva*, the traditional ceremonial center of Pueblo life; nowadays, the conceptions embrace, as well, the instruction of the school, the contemporary center of what they view as the outside world. Pueblo Indian life is the story of these two centers, each symbolic of

---

[9] These words are also on a poster that hangs in the high school administration office.

socializing focal points of their dual-world existence. In terms of impact, is it the *kiva* and the school,[10] equally or to varying extents? The *kiva* or the school? Sometimes the *kiva*, sometimes the school? Neither the *kiva*, nor the school? These alternatives reflect how traditional and nontraditional culture can shape the lives of Pueblo people, depending on the "conceptions of their minds"—depending, that is, on how their culture and personal life experience have defined their sense of who they are and who they can and should be.

THE ROLE OF THE RESEARCHER

My early associations with Indian High school were cordial. I was first brought there by trusted intermediaries who facilitated the necessary introductions; local persons had advised me that in New Mexico personal initiative was not the best way to establish contact. I learned thereafter that to secure access I would have to present myself to the school board and to precede this meeting by submitting a written proposal. Accordingly, I prepared a statement called "Making Life Choices Within a Dual-World Setting." In fact, this statement has oriented my research from beginning to end. In my months of interviews, I explored the range of life choices students make, but concentrated overwhelmingly on the one relating to their schooling, appreciating that this is not a choice quite like choosing to wear a Chicago Bears or Los Angeles Raiders jacket, or deciding to attend Highlands University or New Mexico State.

In this proposal, I also detailed a code of conduct (none of it particularly startling to researchers), an explicit characterization of how I expected to be present in the setting for which school superintendent and school board were the gatekeepers:

1. Researchers should be professionally responsible: Responsibility means trying to make a difference ... for the work of educators and for the children they teach.
2. Researchers do not have a right to be in your school: They enter only with your permission and they stay only with your permission.
3. Researchers are in your school as guests in your home: They must learn how, by your definition, to be properly present.
4. Researchers should be unobtrusive: They do not interfere with the normal work of students, teachers, and administrators.

---

[10]Strictly speaking, these are not equivalent institutions. The *kiva*'s instructional undertakings encompass all tribal members throughout their lives and are rooted essentially in religion. It combines the functions of a church and school.

5. Researchers must [maintain] confidentiality and anonymity at all times.
6. Researchers must be sensitive: They cannot ignore how what they write may affect the people and institutions that grant them the opportunity to conduct their research.

On the occasion of my hearing, the school board members openly discussed their reservations about me and my project. Coming from what obviously was my cultural and geographic distance, I could get them wrong, they thought, misinterpreting and misrepresenting what it means to live in two worlds. In addition, they wondered: Could I do them any good? Would I do them any harm? True, times had changed, but they remembered with considerable displeasure the past work of anthropologists (see, for example, Trimble, 1977). Was I an anthropologist, and, if not, as I said I was not, what was I?

Indian writers are blunt about anthropologists: Paula Gunn Allen (Laguna Pueblo) enthuses, "the more writers we have ... the more Native American people are going to be able to claim themselves and take it back from Hollywood, take it back from the anthropologists. Isn't that exciting?" (quoted in Coltelli 1990:18). And, more forcibly, Gerald Vizenor (Minnesota Chippewa) says: "Anthropologists believe they are right.... I, on the other hand, think that their methodology is narrow, bigoted, and colonial ... and that most of what they say is bullshit ... at very best, bullshit.... They got a bundle of bad methodologies ... " (1990:161).

The Pueblo school board members, and the other Indians working in Indian High School, shared this view of anthropologists. In their eyes, I would have been safer as an agent of the KGB or the Internal Revenue Service. I explained that I was a qualitative researcher,[11] clarified what this means, and listened with relief to the superintendent's summarizing remarks to his school board: we most definitely need to be cautious about the research of a non-Indian outsider, we're venturing on new ground, the board's questions are legitimate, but we need to get good data. There's no money involved (as there was not, for the school) in Peshkin's project, and this could be an opportunity for the school.

I was uneasy throughout this session with the school board, and I depended on the reputation and eloquence of the superintendent to be persuasive beyond anything I could say. For different reasons, I have been worried ever since by Susan Griffin's astute observation, quoted by Richard Restak in his review of her book, *A Chorus of Stone*: "It is a delicate balance telling someone else's story, entering another life, identifying, feeling as this other might have felt, and yet remaining aware that a boundary exists over which one cannot step"

---

[11]For many, this is a difference without distinction. In fact, I am not a trained anthropologist, and never claim to be an anthropologist, either with colleagues or with anyone else who needs to know my professional identification.

(Susan Griffin, quoted by Restak 1992:15). I am, indeed, "telling someone else's story" when I go beyond the cultural confines of my life to explore why schools typically are not places where Indian students enjoy academic success. I do so in order to enter Indian life, "identifying, feeling as this other might have felt,"[12] concerned to grasp why schools are just marginally important, a place students attend, but not with ardor, a place to perform, but not with distinction, a place of potential but not predictable promise. I enter, identify, and feel, aware that I wear shoes, never moccasins; that I attend dances, never dance; that I listen and observe, never as an Indian. "We may as well admit at the outset that almost no white man … is capable of thinking like an Indian; but we can be on guard against obliviousness of that very fact" (White 1942:122). We unavoidably interpret what we learn through the filters of our own lives, but we do this attuned to and informed by the "realities" of those whose lives we strive to understand. As researchers, we can be on guard, check and double check what we learn and write about, and pray for the best, if so inclined. We can conclude by sending a copy of our manuscript before publication to others who can scan with perspective and judgment beyond our own capability.

One day I stopped in a pottery shop at a nearby Pueblo. Mr. Garcia was on duty watching a professional football game on television and selling his wife's wares. "What are you doing in New Mexico?" he wanted to know. I explained. Everything has changed and the country's going to the dogs, he said, so I wouldn't learn anything. Mr. Garcia notwithstanding, I believe I have learned something, but just what it is I have learned, learning considered from whose perspective, and learning of any value for whose purposes—these are matters for this book.

AVOIDING LOGOFIXION

The expectation that research should lead to solutions can be persuasively argued, particularly if the problem researched has substantial bearing on someone's life. Whether or not children and communities benefit from schooling is such a problem. In language that applies quite fully to education, Perri Klass writes convincingly for solutions in studies of poverty: "The study of poverty and its traps must also become the study of ways out, ways around,

---

[12]I would make the same observations about any place I conducted research; this type of understanding is central to all inquiry. The presumption of good intentions implied by this and other approaches to a study do not lead to outcomes that will be acceptable to readers from within the community or institution of study. Perhaps the strongest recent instance of an unacceptable outcome is the vociferous Pueblo reaction to Ramón A. Gutiérrez' book, *When Jesus Came, the Corn Mothers Went Away*. Sylvia Rodriguez elaborates on this reaction in her review of the book (1994: 892–9).

ways through. And, because too much bad news can bring on a sense of fatalism, along with the message of the grim facts ... there sometimes has to be, paradoxically, also the message of hope and resilience" (1992:56). This is the picture on the one hand.

On the other hand, cautions abound. Indian cinematographer David Seals exclaims, "Since when does a whiteman, no matter how well-meaning, tell us what we have to do to make it in America?" (*Powwow Highway* 1991:7). Adds writer Wendy Rose (Hopi-Miwok): "I hate it when other people write about my alienation and anger. Even if it's true. I'm not proud of it. It has crippled me, made me sick, made me out of balance" (1983:253). Finally, Paula Gunn Allen elaborates tellingly through the voice of Ephanie, the main character in her novel: "Do they [non-Indians] call us victims over and over so we will believe it? ... They tell us, over and over, how we have been destroyed. Isn't that how hypnosis works? ... How can we escape the snares of pity? Of smiling, gentle eyes? Of sweet, giving, generous hands?" (1983:159).

Seals, Rose, and Allen persuade me that I must strive to disclose what I have learned in ways that neither offend nor exacerbate what I have seen. They persuade me, in short, to avoid "logofixion"[13] in its several expressions. *To logofy* is to damage with words. Though logofixion, unlike crucifixion, is seldom disastrous, it encompasses a range of meanings and outcomes, some more insidious than others, all of them more annoying than fatal: to write or speak pityingly; to cast as victim; to predict or forecast dire ends; to present uninvited solutions to the problems of others; and to romanticize or to extol, as in creating images of the noble savage, the noble elder, the noble cosmology.

Convinced that I must avoid the hazards of logofixion, I approach writing this book with a touch of timidity. Deciding not to write at all would be a simple solution. I choose to write, intrigued by the stories I have heard, none of them paid for, all of them told by persons who could, if they chose to do so, tell anyone they had met with me (see White below). I am optimistic that I can build a narrative around the stories told to me during hours of interviewing, a narrative that might even be informative to Indian educators and tribal leaders. I add this observation not just in passing but as a reminder that those who permitted me to conduct this study required that it focus on matters of their concern about education at Indian High School.

The writing of anthropologist White instructs in a negative way. His introduction to a monograph on Santa Ana Pueblo acknowledges five points about the conditions of his fieldwork. First, the Santa Anans "zealously guarded the faith of their forefathers"; second, they strive to raise their children to "guard

---

[13]I created this neologism to describe a set of related behaviors that, I thought, otherwise had no name.

the secrets of [their] people, to tell the white man nothing"; third, that this "cultural quarantine" was a most effective means of "guarding their culture"; fourth, that because of this, "the work of the ethnographer suffers ... [and] the ethnologist ... must keep his identity a deep secret"; and, fifth, that "the ethnographer, working incognito..." needs to find Indians who are "willing to help" and "together lay plans to make an ethnographic record ... in strictest secrecy and at considerable distance from the pueblo" (White 1942:9–10). White worked from a then prevailing ethic that, relatively speaking, sanctioned researchers to learn by any means and to disclose at any cost. His respect was directed more to his fellow scholars, less to those whom he studied.

Clearly, the Pueblo communities fear for their physical and cultural survival, but I must not lament this possibility louder than they do. I am motivated to learn and to understand, but not to join a chorus of wailing outsiders that is moved by dread statistics of dropouts, substance abuse, unemployment, or suicide rates. I have tried to see what an outsider can see: I begin with their words and images; they become my own, transformed as I shape my own voice in the process of characterizing and interpreting. I learn of their pains and pleasures. Both proliferate, as is true for all of us.

Pueblo people, young and old, speak readily of historic and contemporary distresses, refusing, it seems, to be determined by them. They speak further of the persistence of joy, creativity, hope, and community, of the persistence of people persisting, which argues strongly against conclusions drawn from the seeming forces of distress. Forewarned by the bristling of Seals, Rose, and Allen, and by the presumptions of White, I seek a path that appropriately recognizes the two worlds I frequented as a non-Indian researcher,[14] while seeking to understand the two worlds of the Pueblo Indian people.

THE RESEARCHER AND SUBJECTIVITY

In his long review of Indian literature, titled "Who Gets to Tell Their Stories," James Kincaid advises that "The first step ... is not to blubber, or to see so easily" (1992:24). Several years ago, having caught myself blubbering (Peshkin 1988), I subsequently reasoned that I would benefit by noting my sentiments as they were elicited in the course of my research process. Thus I recorded them as they emerged. Taken together, my sentiments, or *Subjective-I's*, as I call them, remind me generally of the personal, developmental aspect to the conduct of

---

[14]The following section on subjectivity captures some of my sense of self as I lived through the experience of my fieldwork. Most telling about my dual-world experience as researcher is its transiency. Unlike the Pueblos', mine had a termination date affixed to it.

all research, but also of the cautionary motifs that may arise and have bearing on the process of collecting data, analyzing it, and writing it up.

Hereafter, I describe aspects of my personal journey uncovered in the course of conducting this study. My intent is not the matter of "look at me," but of "look who it is that has come here," the latter of consequence both to my self-awareness as I write, and to informing readers as they consider what my text contains. The self who came to learn about Pueblo school and community soon encountered his Cultural Holocaust-I. This I emerged very early from the frequent talk of group survival I heard. Never before had I met anyone who referred seriously to survival as a contemporary, ongoing, vitally personal issue. Haunted by the horrors of cultural extinction, Indian people live with survival as an enduring condition of their lives. No Jew should be unmoved by this condition, a matter for American Indians of historic fact and current possibility. I believe, moreover, that no one should be unmoved by the matter of survival.

I next encountered the Coopted-I, the result of my agreement with the school board to be sensitive to how I wrote about them, to not inquire about religion, and to submit a draft of my manuscript for their scrutiny before publication. Previously, I felt I had been sensitive; moreover, I had voluntarily sent my manuscripts to school and community leaders prior to publication in the case of earlier projects. What was new for me was the explicit formalizing of this practice in a setting marked by institutionalized secrecy about all matters relating to religion. I detected this Coopted-I when I read monographs that clearly violated Pueblo convictions about secrecy, and also when I began to interview, feeling that it would be inexcusable if I even inadvertently asked a question that was interpretable as digging into religion.

Conquest, domination, defeat, betrayal, disease—these fates pervaded so much of what I read about Indians in the Americas, the stories, as I wrote earlier, that inspired logofixion in non-Indian writers. Tacking between the facts of Indian history and my desire to avoid logofixion, I came to the Perverse-I, who hoped to find a story to tell, not just of a small victory snatched from the clutches of otherwise daily disaster, but of a true triumph, a celebratory accomplishment, verifiable beyond the confines of my possibly magnifying imagination. I yearned for a story free of the despair of the Lakota Sioux (Grobsmith 1981) or the Menomoni (Spindler and Spindler 1971). With this Perverse-I prevailing, I would confound detractors and naysayers of Indian life, the pessimists of both worlds.

I sit in class one day at Indian High School and notice a tall, athletic-looking student. I realize, as I look at her, that I know what she does in her free time and during vacations, what tribes her mother and father come from, how her mother and father met, what responsibilities her father has in his tribal affairs, and what his previous jobs were from the time he left high school to the present. I further realize that every afternoon when I drive home from out-of-town, I listen to National Native News, a program directed to Indian affairs throughout the nation, and that when I read or tune in to radio or television programs, I instantly attend to anything related to Indians. Thus when Roger Welch, in his *Sunday Morning* "Postcard from Nebraska," speaks warmly of pioneers in covered wagons, the settlers who traversed the Oregon Trail, I listen (vainly) for his equally warm awareness of the Indians his settlers were unsettling.

I had come to a combination Immersed/Caring-I, a familiar one, the product of bringing into sharp focus the people and place I had come to learn about and, relatively speaking, of blurring almost everything else around me in my life. This degree of immersion goes along with caring about the people and the place. In the compass of my caring are a considerable investment of self, and all that this entails: the people and place I was immersed in had become important in and to my life. The caring is compounded by the extensive time and cooperation I receive, indispensable conditions for the success of my work, that of the uninvited researcher who moves into the domain of others, and who clearly needs and depends upon them. How could I not care about people who literally make possible any success I enjoy!

And how could I not be more than ordinarily concerned whether or not my writing was going to contribute to what Indians already believe is the abundance of writing that, good intentions notwithstanding, gets them wrong, misstates, and overstates, ad infinitum. One day a recent graduate of Indian High School came back from college for a visit. She and I discussed a new book about Indians that we both had read. Not bad, in general, she said, but in the end, the author does not get things straight. It is one more of "those" books. Hers was one of many such comments that in one way or another made the same point: non-Indian writers do us wrong.

Getting things straight, as defined by others, seldom is easy. Whose idea of straight is the right one? Given 19 tribes and varying points of view within each tribe, the challenge mounts. Though this problem is not peculiar to research among Indians, I am concerned not to add to the already existing feeling of being denigrated.

Thus I came to another subjective disposition, the Fair-I. It derives from living in a society that in regard to human difference oversucceeds in giving offense, in simplifying—if you've known one, you've known them all. It derives from a society that at one level responds with political correctness to difference, a smarmy playing at doing, saying, and writing the right thing, that is careful to avoid giving offense, except in safe company. At another level, it responds with policies and practices of multiculturalism and diversity that brim with good intentions to acknowledge difference and react to it appropriately.

My Fair-I most definitely finds fault with American society for its historic and current unkindness, insensitivity, and injustice to many minority people. But it acknowledges as well that those who have been victimized are not necessarily persons who either live like victims or deserve to be blamed for whatever misfortunes they suffer. Still, hanging an albatross of "the damaged ones" around the necks of a people is to deny them efficacy, autonomy, and responsibility. Thus I want to have it both ways: to affirm the damage while not casting Pueblo people as the walking wounded, though many are.

I want others who learn about Pueblo people from my writing to know them as American people, like others throughout this land, but not to expect a prefatory, normalizing descriptor—"like most parents everywhere" or "like most students everywhere"—whenever I refer to them in some way. In fact, however, it is their difference that I capitalize on in this book, their intended, explicit cultural difference that in its encounter with the whiteman's school contributes to the unintended outcome—modest academic success—that frames my inquiry. It is Pueblo efficacy, autonomy, and responsibility that forms the basis of my speculations (in chapter 6, this volume) about their future as it relates to school and community.

Finally, I came to the Whiteman-I, the reaction to my respondents' frequent references to the whiteman's world; to their boundary setting of our discourse, so I could never forget my cloistering spotlight; to their sense of self defined, in part, by opposition to white others they perceived to be materialistic, time-obsessed, and wasteful. This feeling was reinforced by an observation in Anthony Stevens' book *On Jung*. Carl Jung is quoted as having heard a Pueblo tribal leader say about white Americans: "See how cruel the whites look.... Their lips are thin, their noses sharp.... Their eyes have a staring expression; they are always seeking something. What are they seeking? ... We do not know what they want. We do not understand them. We think they are mad [because] they think with their heads.... We think here [with our hearts]" (*New York Times Book Review* 1991:43). Never before had I occasion to think of myself as a whiteman, an antagonizing, villainous other, and one who could be stigmatized for being a researcher.

The explicit focus of this book is on Pueblo Indians and their self-stated urgent need for cultural survival. The implicit focus is on the many people in this country and around the world who confront a juggernaut of social change that promises to sweep away all but the most superficial aspects of their cultural distinctiveness and, thus, their cherished individual and collective identity. So challenged, the beleaguered group struggles with the often contradictory demands of cultural maintenance and cultural change, of remaining in some form, to some degree who they have been and are today, and becoming who they want and need to be. Often, they are neither free nor willing to sacrifice one for the other. Their burden is not lightened by readily available models of others who managed wisely to meet this dual challenge, or by a manual of procedure, a how-to-do-it guide to simultaneously remaining and becoming. Their struggle is a story of the human condition, one that is instructed, however mysteriously, even by proverbial wisdom: "Whoever forsakes the old way for the new, knows what he is losing but not what he will find" (quoted in Ferraro 1993).

Pueblo concerns for remaining focus on the cultural forms of their tribal community, in general, and of the *kiva*, in particular, the religious center of traditional tribal life. Community and *kiva* are places of enduring importance enshrined in individual and collective memory. This is memory of consequence, bred in Pueblo bones, holding structures of meaning that underlie Pueblo life. Pueblo concerns for becoming focus on the cultural forms of Anglo society and the whiteman's school. They are places of lesser importance and disturbing memory.

2

Education at Indian High School: Good Intentions

ORIENTATIONS

Before the new academic year begins for students, Superintendent Valdez meets in his office with his administrators, from the heads of the dormitories, cafeteria, and kitchen to the principals of the middle and high schools. For the most part, this is a roomful of Indian men and women. The superintendent is a Pueblo man; most of the staff are Pueblo people. School policy is oriented toward hiring Indians in all positions.

The meeting opens with a prayer in English by one of the Pueblo tribal governors, a longtime employee of the school: "I talk to my canes,"[1] he begins, "for daily guidance. I ask the Great Spirit for daily guidance. As tribal leader, I'm mother and father to all members of my tribe." He continues to pray, creating a mood of caring, of somber concern for the well-being of students and their tribes. Following the governor's prayer, the superintendent presents his charge for the year: to establish an Indian school, not just one attended by Indian children. To him this means taking the school's educative "experience in an Indian direction twenty-four hours a day, seven days a week." He wants the students to pray more, to feel there is support for them to be traditional in their general conduct at school, and to see their behavior as right or wrong "in terms of tribal community expectations." What the *community* says, what the *community* wants, what the *community* needs—throughout the school year that follows, this Indianizing theme will resound, notwithstanding that it is directed to education in a whiteman's school, an institution of the non-Indian world.

---

[1] The governors of each of the 19 tribes received canes from President Lincoln in recognition of their political authority. The canes are passed on from governor to governor.

26

The high school principal picks up this theme for her orientation of several newly employed teachers. "We are accountable to the 19 Pueblo governors," she informs them early on, leaving no doubt about the school's political and cultural context. Though non-Pueblo Indians are welcome and do attend Indian High School, this federal government school operates under the official banner of the Pueblo tribes, a circumstance of consequence to be understood and appreciated by all school employees, one so central that it is incorporated in the school's mission statement.

She continues her orientation by working through the central terms of the Indian High School Mission Statement: that the school experience be oriented to a "continuous awakening and nurturing" that draws on the central Pueblo values of "respect, harmony and hard work" so that students will make "fulfilling life choices in an Indian and non-Indian world." Having located the school's thrust in general terms, she adds that the students, as adults, are likely to sit on their tribe's administrative councils. This obligates the school to ready them "to handle the issues they will face," which means that teachers must integrate the school's regular curriculum with everything that can be taken from Indian history, culture, and contemporary life. Appreciating that this is a tall order, the principal reassures the new teachers that they will get support with the task of integration, and they should not "push it so fast you become anxious."

Within a week of the new-teacher orientation, the superintendent addresses parents who are present on campus to drop off their children for the opening of classes. Parents become familiar with this trip to school, as each Friday afternoon they come by to take their children home, and each Sunday afternoon they return to drop them off. On this particular Friday, many stay on for this session with the superintendent. He confirms that they have made a good choice in sending their children to Indian High School, and he reminds them that the school cannot succeed without their support. The superintendent returns to another theme, the necessity of education: "If we're to succeed as Indian people, if we're to get our fair share, we must have good education. We must be disciplined—to get up early, to study hard, to do what we need to do. Then we'll win." He closes his presentation with a request that the parents "remember us in your prayers."

As the school year progresses, these same thoughts are repeated in the presentations of administrators, teachers, and dormitory staff. In time, none of the thoughts will be unfamiliar; if called upon, students will be able to recite them, if not grasp their meaning and implications. A full picture of the school's values is included in the Indian High School handbook that each student receives, its statement of "philosophy" reflecting familiar imagery. Students are informed that their school "is a place where my people's values are as precious as rain on a dry day," where students develop the "inner strength to become a leader in any path I walk," at a time in their lives when they explore "new paths," while always remembering "to remain true to my Indian self." The statement of philosophy closes with the school's own version of becoming and remaining: "There is a larger society, a larger world in which I must learn to live and survive, but I must never forget who I am and where I am from."

When, some time later, the superintendent addresses the entire student group, his language on this occasion is not of precious rain on dry days, but of "here's our reality and here are your responsibilities":

> Our economic situation is the worst in New Mexico. Sometimes we feel insignificant about the concerns of the country, but when it comes to Indian people, the Indian School and its students can make a difference. We need to stimulate our students to accept responsibility, to understand the complexity of the world, and to learn to make a difference. As you go out to compete with other people, arm yourself with who you are as Indian people. I want the Indian School to have made a difference. That's what I want people to say about us.

The superintendent wants his students to make a difference in the lives of their people, and his school to be a factor in making this happen. His Pueblo constituents support this aspiration.

Thus, by the time students finish high school, they have been compelled to heed messages from their several worlds about responsibility and necessity, service and survival, tradition and change. Such messages are to be expected from school and tribal leaders whose positions make them more than ordinarily aware of the tribes' internal and external circumstances and needs. Such awareness clearly extends to parents, teachers, and students, as I learn from their reflections and recollections.

Desi Rivera, for example, speaks eloquently on these matters. She is wife, mother, worker, and dedicated traditional tribal member. She does not shy away from either of the dual paths she and her children encounter, seeming, rather, to revel in the promise of each. She speaks here of her Indian world:

> It was not too long ago when my parents made a remark to our children. "Grandchildren," they said, "when you grow up, who will you marry?" To my parents, that is important for them to know now. My husband and I waited to listen what their responses were going to be. My kids turned around and told their grandma and grandpa, "We don't know who we are going to marry, but we are going to marry an Indian." I could see the smile on my dad's face. Mom and I talk. If we want to continue to be Indian, and if we want our children to be Indian, to take part, to know and respect our ways, then that is what we need to do [marry an Indian]. Golly, how would I ever have known [this would happen], my parents telling me what their parents told them when they were growing up. And now I am telling my children, and they are in turn talking to their grandparents. It was

just reinforcing that what they shared with me as a small child is planted here. It didn't go in one ear and out the other.

Desi is comforted by her children's response to her parents' question about choice of mates, pleased that her own traditional values seem to have taken root, as she hoped they would. Then she considers the matter of her children's schooling, triggered by recent newspaper accounts of a new, well-endowed prep school for Indian youth proposed to be built nearby. Would she send her children there?

> If my children fit into the caliber of students [who would attend such an academically elite school], I would have no problem. I want the best for my kids. I want them to have the opportunities I had. If there are greater opportunities, I would say yes to them. Because I know that as I raised them, they'll always know where their heart is, and that's within their Pueblo. We've told them what we feel. It wouldn't do for me as a parent to shortchange my children for being the individuals that they want to be. I'd never be fearful for them not knowing who they are.

Desi and others simultaneously reach inside for their values and seek outside for the means to realize their personal and communal aspirations, tied both to the traditional world of remaining, and to the dominant world of becoming.

Most Indian High School students return home each weekend to their families at the reservation. To be sure, as in communities everywhere, there are troubled families, indifferent families, and uncaring families who ignore their children's life at school. For many, however, the weekend at home is an occasion for them to discuss school. One or the other or all of a student's grandparents, parents, older siblings, and aunts and uncles will ask: "How are you doing?" "How are your grades?" "Have you been good?" "What's going on in school?" "Do I need to sign anything?" Seniors get pointed inquiries ("What's going on with your college applications or your scholarships?" "What are you going to do after graduation?") and pointed encouragement ("Make better grades, then you'll get more money for college." "You're a smart person. You'll do good when you go to college." "Stay out of trouble and strive so you can graduate. You're almost there, don't give up, and keep on praying."). It is hard to give up, say the students, "because you have everybody out pressuring you to keep on trying."

Though not strictly a college-prep school, Indian High School strongly orients its students toward college, but not to the exclusion of other postsecondary school and work possibilities. The school employs a full-time college-career counselor who concentrates on all phases of the college-going process, including test-taking, information about colleges and universities, visits to institutions with a special interest in Indian students, filling out applications, seeking scholarships, and, not least, moral support. The efforts of this counselor are reflected in the school's daily bulletins. In September, juniors are invited to learn more about the Air Force Academy, the Naval Academy, and West Point—"High grades and high test scores are needed to be considered for the Academies." Also in September, seniors are informed that if they do not complete career data sheets, they won't receive "college materials related to your interests" and that ACT/SAT achievement test deadlines are coming so they should "check with your parents this weekend regarding test fees." In November, students are told in regard to next month's ACT Test, "I will check your completed form and assist you if you need help but you need to get the form to me by the above date." In April, students are alerted to the chance to learn "more about Harvard/Radcliffe University" by attending a meeting at the Career Center. Also in April, by which time students may have reached a decision about their post-graduation plans, seniors going to New Mexico State University learn that Angela Mora "will be on campus" to help them with applications, aid, housing, etc.

Orientations toward college are reflected in a teacher's classroom comments, often about learning how to take notes as a skill students must have for their college classes. In an English class, the teacher says, "OK, so, if in college someone asks who set things up for telling the stories in *Canterbury Tales*, people will say Chaucer, but you know better. You know it was the host." Another English teacher says, "We'll work on tone and style of writing. Also higher-order thinking. You need to be patient with me and yourself. Some of you are as stubborn as hell, but I see improvements. Autobiographies are coming up. You'll need them for [college] applications." And the after-school study director, who works with select students who are trained and usually paid to assist younger students with their school work, tells a group of these student aides that even though they approached her too late to be paid, they should serve as volunteer tutors because it will look good on their college applications.

A bright new teacher characterizes his fellow teachers in terms that are consistent with the views of older teachers who have taught much longer at Indian High School: "I think the staff here is very dedicated; people try very hard. I think there's a high level of professionality. They have a very low turnover, and there's a certain community-family feeling among faculty." Nothing I observed and nothing I heard from students contradicted this view of teachers. Overall, they appear to enjoy teaching Indian youth, take pleasure in their close contact with Indian culture, and believe they find rewards teaching at Indian High School that they would not find elsewhere.

According to data assembled by educators at Indian High School in the 1990–1991 school year, 52% of their 54 teachers had earned a master's degree or higher (comparable figures for all public schools in Albuquerque and Santa Fe were 51% and 50% respectively); they had an average of 10.3 years teaching experience (compared with 11.6 in Albuquerque's and 13.6 in Santa Fe's public schools); and 33% of the faculty were Indian (compared with 5% in Albuquerque and 6% in Santa Fe). In fact, Indian High School has a higher percentage of Indian teachers than any other high school in the entire state.

THE AMERICAN CURRICULUM

Given a school administered by an all-Pueblo school board, a Pueblo superintendent who is committed to establishing an Indian school, a faculty that is one-third Indian, and an all-Indian student population, what does the school experience look like at Indian High School? Consider a teacher's classroom rules, a one-page list of *do*'s and *don't*s that she distributes to her classes on the first day of school:

1. No food, drinks, or gum allowed.
2. Respect yourself, others, and their property.
3. Have a positive attitude.
4. Come to class prepared and ready to work.
5. Behave properly at all times.
6. Clean up after yourself.
7. Do your work.
8. You must have a pass to leave the classroom.
9. Stay in your seat until you are dismissed.

By the lights of this prototypically American set of guidelines, she could be teaching almost anywhere in the country. After all, Indian High School, as an American school attended by American youth,[2] bears the hallmarks of American educational universals. Here is what they look like in the school's classrooms and activities.

In Advanced Drafting, the teacher circulates around the room, helping students with their work. Students work alone, sitting on stools, the tools of their work arrayed on their tilted desks. When they complete an assignment, the teacher grades it exactly, taking off points for erasures, double lines,

---

[2]I've made similar statements based on fieldwork in other school settings. Though American schools can be different in important ways, they share a range of common forms and activities.

sloppy printing, using light lines when dark lines are required, missing technical details. This teacher has a fairly precise standard for judging the quality of work.

Spanish classes present a different picture. The teacher, in up-to-date fashion, speaks almost nothing but Spanish, even though it is an introductory class. In a smooth, steady flow of language, she works from exercise to explanation, pointing, gesturing, demonstrating, so that students can connect sound with meaning. She concludes the period with an *examencito*. This is an eighth-period class and the teacher's words compete with the grunting sounds of the football team warming up that pour through the open windows.

Ninth graders in their civics class read an article about the American family in the latest edition of *Scholastic Update*. From talk about questions related directly to the article they bridge easily to an overview of TV families. One student condemns the Cosbys as "too perfect; they have an answer for everything." Many think *Roseanne* is better, and like *Blossom* best of all because, as one student puts it, a "single-parent family is realistic." Sometime later the teacher struggles to draw students into discussion of the then raging Anita Hill–Clarence Thomas controversy; students sit mute, unwilling or unable to get into a discussion of ideas regarding the validity of Hill's charge of sexual abuse or the worthiness of Thomas to sit on the Supreme Court. This topic is far removed from their daily lives. When the teacher tells about a Colorado man who grew a record-size pumpkin, the class becomes animated about the prospects of organizing a pumpkin-carving contest as part of a Halloween party with apple bobbing and wearing scary costumes.

Advanced Placement English follows an outline of assignments for the week: Monday—critical thinking exercises; Tuesday—timed writing; Wednesday—direct instruction on grammar; Thursday—reading assignment and analysis; and Friday—essay due on "Do you agree with the author's attitude about football?" "When you write your essays," the teacher warns, "watch out for passive voice." Inspired by several poems the students are reading, the teacher muses on their emphasis that: "Life is short. We could write some good papers about that. You are young and think you have a lot of time. Why do old people talk about the past? Because that's all they have. Why do we always ask you to write about your goals? Because you have a future." As the school year ends, this teacher and others will note the item in the daily announcements that tells "Senior Teachers: Please submit any 'F' grades for Senior students . . . failing a class may cause a senior to be ineligible to graduate and parents will need to be notified."

Out-of-class opportunities include a predictable set of activities. Within the first weeks of the school year, students learn with pleasure that yearbooks will be distributed in the Old Gym, about the same time that all athletic and club participants are told of the timetable for picture taking for the forthcoming yearbook. For another early-in-the-year event, selection of class officers, the senior class sponsor congratulates the newly elected officers for winning and the class for its wise choices: "Let's have a great year." This election is soon followed by voting for student council members, one representative from each of 28 home rooms, who will attend biweekly meetings from September through May.

Fund raising goes on all school year, as Indian High School students join their fellows across the country in a splurge of selling everything their peers might find irresistible. "Staff/students: Say 'Thank you' to someone special. The National Honor Society is selling 'Thank You Grams.'" Indian High School students are not denied experience with that special extracurricular combination of fun, money-raising, and volunteerism that so many school activities entail: "Joy of Giving Dance sponsored by Student Council on Sunday. Make a good Christmas come true. Toys, canned goods, or clothes for those who are less fortunate. It's the Gift of Giving. Thanks."

Nor are they denied their place in the athletic sun. Indian High School students (and their parents) dearly love sports. No special occasion is required for students to play pick-up basketball games on the school's outdoor courts at any time of the day, much to the consternation of teachers whose classrooms abut the courts. Organized team sports for female and male students shape the entire school year; there is never an in-between time. Indian High School teams have been state champions in basketball, football, track, and baseball.

One chilly, mid-October Saturday morning, a lone boy walks around the track that circles the football field across from my house. I have just finished running laps. The boy is the cheerleading squad's only male member. Finished walking, he sits on a bench, one of two on the sidelines set up for the football team, near where players and coaches more usually stand and watch the unfolding of the team's fate on the playing field. This year, the team has excelled, for the afternoon's game will decide the district championship. The lone boy is joined by two female cheerleaders. They walk around the track, huddled shoulder to shoulder beneath a large blanket, chilled by the still brisk morning air. When all cheerleaders arrive, they practice for the afternoon's game. From the outside, I see any school's cheerleaders in practice; any team's time of decision for determining a championship; any coach's pride in his player's achievement; any player's nervousness in anticipation of the big game; any student's delight in the vicarious pleasures of the game as seen from the sidelines and the stands. The program distributed to each ticket purchaser contains the roster for each team: name, class, position, height, weight, and jersey number. In addition, each Indian High School player is identified by tribe: Robert Rodriguez—Santo Domingo, Sam Gonzales—Jemez, Tim Guadalupe—Laguna, Tony Garcia—Tesuque, Frank Valdez—Picuris, and so forth. A legacy of the Spanish conquest is the enduring use of Spanish names throughout their lives. A distinction of the school is that students are known by their tribal affiliation.

Of course, more than sports and related events fill a student's out-of-class time. The school's daily announcements chronicle the variety of available opportunities: "Soviet exchange students and new applicants: Meet in my classroom. Bring your Uzbek pen pal photo and letter." "Students: Get your tux for the prom at a 15% discount. See Martin for details." "Seniors: Please come to Catherine's room for cap and gown fitting on Monday." "Staff/students: Send/bring your end-of-year paper to Room 101 for recycling." And to end the year on the right note, the school's Student Rights and Responsibilities Office includes a cautionary note on the next-to-last day of the school year:

> Students: IMPORTANT! NOW IS NOT THE TIME TO GET INTO TROUBLE!!
> There will not be any type of Disorderly Activities (i.e., Water Fights, Shaving Cream attacks, etc.) allowed . . . Be creative and think of more positive ways to celebrate the end of school!

A representation of what is commonplace in schools across the country easily could be extended. The experience of performance standards, quizzes, current events, college readiness, fundraising, and athletic competition is but a limited listing of "the American curriculum" that, to one degree or another, all our schools share. However, the nation's tradition of local control affords local communities the prerogative to move beyond what is common and to place their own cultural stamp on the school experience.

THE INDIANIZED CURRICULUM

Indian High School bears the hallmarks, however less deeply rooted in school practice, of Indian educational particulars. I learn about some version of these particulars in response to a general question I ask wherever I go to study a school and its host community—"What differences follow from the fact of whose children attend a certain school?" In his early-in-the-semester address to students, the superintendent advises them, "Before you take on a new challenge, you need to assess your strengths. One of your strengths is that you are Indian. Those of you who practice your culture, your religion, will continue to do so here." This refers to what he hopes students will do informally, on their own, within the time and place of their five days and nights spent at Indian High School. Given Pueblo values, it does not refer to religion becoming a formal part of the curricular experience. However, Indian High School recently hired a full-time curriculum specialist to promote the formal integration of the curriculum with all that is allowable from Indian culture. I call this integrating process *Indianization.*[3]

I walk through Indian High School corridors, attend classes, note what adorns its walls and bulletin boards, observe meetings, and collect documents in order to see the signs of Indianization. I don't mean to evaluate its effectiveness or judge the sincerity of any teacher's efforts (or lack of them). I look, rather, for the presence of effort, its nature and scope, pleased to acquire evidence of its outcomes, as and if it turns up.

In an Indian High School in-house publication, the principal defined and set forth a rationale for the "Indian perspective." "Indian perspective," she wrote, "is an overall approach to the entire operation of the school program which reflects Indian points of views, values and behavior." The specific areas of application are the subject matter of the formal curriculum, how students are taught, the activities of the informal curriculum, and the "school's organizational structure, values, and policies." Specifically, the latter area of application includes the school calendar, which should reflect "Indian religious days, as opposed to Columbus Day." In addition, "There should be Indian preference policies, competent Indians to serve as role models . . . [and] buy-Indian contracts for goods and services. . . . [T]here should be schoolwide expectations on how Tribal leaders, parents, and elders are treated." Given this mandate, teachers, administrators, and staff are encouraged to Indianize all that they do in their roles as Indian High School employees. I expect to see its manifestations wherever I look; for the most part, I do.

Earlier, I referred to the principal's orientation of new teachers by introducing them to the Indian values in the school's mission statement. This effort is supported by many of the school's weekly in-service programs, some of them devoted exclusively to the process of Indianization. One school project, Ventures in Computer Technology, offered $100 incentives to teachers with creative ideas for using computers in their classrooms, and an extra $25 for "Lessons that include both computer use and Indian perspective objectives."

A counterpart to pre-school orientations provided to new and veteran Indian High School teachers is one organized for the many dormitory staff. They are responsible for the students from the time school is out each afternoon until

---

[3]In his discussion of the achievement of minority students, Erickson calls such curricular efforts "culturally responsive pedagogy" (1993:48). What I call *Indianization* McLaughlin (1992) refers to as an "indigenized" school, in his study of Mesa Valley Community School on the Navajo Reservation. Philip's exploration (1983) of communication practices carefully documents cultural differences among Warm Springs Indian Reservation students with implications for grade school classrooms.

breakfast the next morning. The staff are important persons in the students' academic and personal affairs. They attend a talk given by a Santa Clara educator organized around a series of slides showing Indian art objects. He discusses each slide, but he elaborates the implications of the last slide in his set that shows a figure with a split head. This symbolizes, he says, that Indians live in two worlds, and that students are trying to bring the two worlds together in their own lives. Someone asks the speaker to consider the "inconsistencies and inadequacies of Indian students compared to non-Indians." He answers that "for Indian people, [non-Indian] education is very new. We're adapting, but it takes a long time. We're looking at models of education not of our own making; its standards and ideals are not our own. Students become apathetic about the sixth grade, reflecting the conflict between home and school."

Indian High School admits students from non-Pueblo tribes, but as a Pueblo-run institution it gives preference to Pueblo students. Most students pay a nominal tuition of $50 per semester, or nothing if they cannot afford this amount. The Indian High School admissions director, a Pueblo tribal leader and graduate of Indian High School, sees the school as an adjunct to Indian life. In his interview with new applicants, he conveys his personal outlook, as represented below in his recollection of how an interview might proceed:

> Toward the end I say, "Are you proud of who you are?" They say, "What do you mean?" [I say,] "You are a Native American. Are you proud to be one?" They say, "Yes." I say, "I am asking because this man is proud of who he is and what he is, and I just wanted you to know that. And if you haven't started thinking about it, you can't forget that you are Native American. You are coming for academics; you need that to survive in the world tomorrow. But you can't forget your language and your dancing."

Students will see and hear much that reminds them that they are Native Americans. In 1991, the school developed a project called "Competency Testing for Indian Students: A Cultural Approach." This project arose out of the state's compulsory competency test. Indian High School leaders reasoned that their students should be tested by state standards but also to meet "competencies needed not only in the outside world but the 'Indian World,' as well." To this end, Indian High School developed 19 cultural competencies, "as defined by tribal leaders, elders, parents, and students," which all graduates should acquire. The list includes knowledge of tribal political structures; jurisdictional issues relating to "social, water and land rights"; tribal sovereignty and self-determination; Indian history; current issues; value differences "between the Indian and non-Indian worlds"; and "critical" issues faced by Native Americans, such as "alcoholism, suicide, unemployment" (the deep shadows in Pueblo family and community life).

Backing up the acquisition of these 19 competencies is the school library. One-fourth of its total collection is devoted to American Indians; one-half of the books students check out are about American Indians. The library has a handout that lists the call number for everything related to American Indians, from 970.1, History, General, to 970.68, Literature, Poetry, Speeches. Only in such a school would I find the catalog of the Grey Owl Indian Craft Company located in Queens Village, New York, with its offering of Hair Roach Bases, Totemic Prints, and imitation buffalo or elk teeth.

It would be too much to suggest that a distinctly Pueblo system of discipline has been established at the school, but I caught a semblance of one from talking with a staff member who happened upon an incident. A boy had just been teasing some girls by opening their bathroom door. She stopped to speak with him, but he ignored her and walked away. "I hollered at him, 'You get back here. I'm talking to you.' He came to me and I told him what he had done wrong. Another thing, I said, 'You might wonder how come I'm telling you. Remember, you were told that we're like a family at this school. So we here as staff are your parents. I'm your mom and I can tell you.'" That's the way it was at home when she was growing up—adults taking responsibility for the right conduct of children other than their own.[4] She was very pleased to relate this story, pleased with herself for taking the initiative, and pleased with the chance to have acted in a traditional way. After she spoke to him, the misbehaving boy "hit the nearby fountain. I looked at him and he looked at me and he goes, 'I'm sorry.' I said, 'Thank you,' and he walked away."

Graduation ceremonies, an important event in Pueblo families, attract many parents, relatives, and other visitors. All seniors wear traditional Indian clothing for this special occasion. Pueblo and other Indian speakers dominate the program. Graduation is held in a large, outdoor amphitheater, and thus is exposed to the uncertainties of weather. At Indian High School, such uncertainties are conceivably controlled. "I am really a true believer of my way of life," a staff member told me as preface to recounting his recent meeting with Superintendent Valdez on the eve of graduation.

He said, "George, you know, the nuns called me from St. Theresa's School, and they said, 'Mr. Valdez, would you like to borrow our Saint Joseph, because you can light a candle and it will give you clear weather'" [for graduation ceremonies]. The superintendent says, "Sister, I have three or four former governors who

---

[4]According to Suina and Smolkin: "Teaching and learning in the more traditional Pueblos remain in the hands of old Pueblo members. . . . Corrections for inappropriate behaviors may be supplied at any time, in any place within the village, and for any type of unsuitable action" (1994: 117).

work here and they do wonders just as well." So I said, "Mr. Valdez, are you requesting, or what are you saying? I have already got it in my mind; tomorrow morning I will say my prayers." When I say my prayers, I say, "We need rain, we need the snow, or whatever. But graduation is going to be a happy occasion. We wish to have nice sunshine or a few clouds, but no rain. Maybe six this evening, you may give us what you want."

George's prayers for suitable graduation weather point up the special role that Indian employees play at the school. As speakers of the vernacular, for example, they can and do reinforce its use among students by speaking with them in Keres or Tewa. "I use a lot of switching," says a teacher, "English and Indian." He uses his skill with the vernacular to learn if a student is genuinely shy, uninformed, or possibly uncertain about his English language skills.

Moreover, Indian teachers can raise questions in class with an authenticity not available to non-Indians:

> How can we as Native Americans help other Native Americans? How can we get from here to there? How can we offer more jobs? How can we balance what we're learning now and at the same time take part in our culture? How many of you take part in your culture? How many are thinking about taking part in your culture? How many of you know your language? Are you going to dance on your feast day?

"I ask all kinds of questions like that," says a social studies teacher. So did the teachers I observed some years ago at a fundamentalist Christian school. They were fitting questions, since the teachers lived by and taught the orthodoxy in whose name the school had been created.

Indian teachers can stamp authenticity on the concerns they bring to the post-graduation prospects of their students. To be sure, teachers, at their best, care about what becomes of their students; less often are student and teacher linked to the same future: "I can talk with my ninth grade class—there are leaders there. Not everyone is born that way or leans that way. We are crossing our fingers and maybe ten years down the line we will start seeing these kids that will be the leaders in the future." The depth of this teacher's concern builds on the fact that his own future is directly at stake in the conduct of his students.

Moreover, because the Indian teachers live the issues that confront Pueblo communities, they bring certain elements of reality to grasping the aspirations of the school. All teachers heard Superintendent Valdez consider the need of the Pueblos for highly qualified professionals. Non-Indian teachers can comprehend his point about the tribes using their own tribal people to negotiate with state and federal agencies. Indian teachers may convey this point with more force; it is their land and their water that is under negotiation.

Furthermore, they can attend to the subtle and not so subtle aspects of Pueblo tradition, the product of their own sense of historic injustice and their recognition of what they, too, had experienced as adolescents: "[Tradition] is terribly complex. It is a subject that they [students] deal with and I try to help them with in my classes. I think they struggle with it and they have no words. They have to struggle with it and put it into words so it can be a little easier."

Indian teachers also can place what their students are studying within what they see as a suitable context, as did a teacher whose class had been reading a story about "this guy who feels so guilty for everything."

> I said to them, "You know, part of this guy's culture is to feel guilty for everything. A lot of white people grow up in a culture where [they learn that] they're supposed to feel guilty for everything." It's kind of weird because native people don't grow up with that. I said, "If you'll notice, most of the things the guy feels guilty about have to do with nature, or his own nature, and that's something Indian people take as being part of life." That's how I try to help them see that maybe sometimes what they don't understand [in their reading] has to do with the difference in cultures.

If the Indian teachers as Indians bring to their work unique qualifications, all teachers generally have insights, awareness, and sensitivity that develop from their work in a high school within an Indian cultural setting.[5] By one means or another, teachers learn, for example, that their students will be most ready to learn from them if they have established a personal relationship with them. Teachers speak of this relationship as a condition for learning to occur. They learn that they should not single out high-achieving students by holding up their work as exemplary: "It's OK if you privately say, 'May I make a copy of your answer and put it on an overhead, but I won't put your name on it?' The kids will privately feel that sense of accomplishment, but no one will know who it was." They learn that students may request a few minutes of silence before a test, and that this use of silence has it roots in Pueblo culture. "When I was looking at how to make my classroom environment more comfortable, some of the kids brought up that they would like to have a few moments of silence."

---

[5]Indian High School educators have conducted research on Indian learning styles and presented their findings in annual workshops. While some were aware of the work of Au (1986), Jordan (1984), John-Steiner and Osterreich (1975), Philips (1983), and Tharp and Gallimore (1988), drawn from research on Native Hawaiian and Native American children, Indian High School teachers overall did not systematically study and seek to adapt the outcomes in their classrooms.

They learn that when a student has been missing class at long and regular intervals, this student is not necessarily cutting class but possibly is in training for a tribal position. Accommodating such absences is expected of the teachers, though the student is held responsible for class assignments. More typical are short-term student absences as requested by a student's governor, involving all students from a particular tribe. Non-Indian teachers learn that the young man or woman sitting before them in class, who struggles to understand a character, a theme, a rule of grammar, may "in their own communities be bright and shining stars." Says a non-Indian teacher, "What I'm teaching them they may see as totally irrelevant to their lives. The only reason that I had given them that information [in her lessons] at all is so that they can cope in this world, the white world. I don't have to be able to do both, but they do if they want their world to survive. And that's why they come to school at all."

Indian High School teachers need to learn about tabooed topics, those matters that intrude on some aspect of Pueblo culture and thus are not acceptable in Indian High School. The taboos generally relate to religion, in one way or another. For example, teachers may not refer to *kachinas*, though some tribes are distinctly more comfortable than others with public reference to them, and some tribes make them to sell as art objects. Teachers do not assign Tony Hillerman mysteries because of their reference to *kachinas*. Students may censor their own reading if it contains reference to sensitive objects: "I forgot the book, but it said a lot of things, like how our *kachinas* come. We read that book, but I didn't read the whole thing because I didn't want to. My uncle told me not to read it." She referred to things mentioned in other assigned books that "they should never be in there because that's our culture. Sometimes I feel scared to read certain parts." Indian teachers may share this student's perspective: "Hopis, as far as *kachinas*, they're more open. They're allowed to draw them, to paint them, to make *kachina* dolls and sell them. Now, the other Pueblos, even me, when I say 'kachina' . . . you're not even supposed to say it. In my tribe, it's a no-no."

Teachers know that they can't assign Frank Waters's prize-winning novel, *The Man Who Killed the Deer* (1970) because it describes religious practices in a way that disturbs some Pueblos. If a work of literature refers to "touchy subjects like owls or snakes or death," teachers will clarify their presence so that students see them as just a part of the text, and not at all connected to their tribal life. Students may be reluctant to discuss death, as a teacher learned when she was taking attendance and noted that a student was absent. When she asked if anyone knew about him, a student came up to her and said, "'I need to talk with you.' He told me that the absent boy had died over the weekend. I didn't know if we should talk about it. I wanted to because to me this is something we need to talk about, the fact that we've lost someone in our class. Another student said to me, 'Just go on with the normal lesson.' Everybody's head was down."

Next in this odyssey of expressions of Indianness at Indian High School is the academic program, beginning with what is easy to do, but nonetheless deserves mention—placing items on bulletin boards and walls. Just past the entrance to one of the academic buildings I see these messages:

Culture comes from within the circle ... starting with the elders. *IHS Competency #12 Respect for Elders*	Children are creatures of God, born with a potential that must be developed by schools as a basic responsibility. *Mr. Valdez, Supt. IHS*	There is a larger society, a larger world in which I must learn to live and survive. But I must never forget who I am and where I am from.
The secret of education lies in respecting the pupil.	Survival of our Indian people is directly related to the education of our people. *Sara Jiminez IHS Principal*	Know the difference between the Indian and the non-Indian world. *IHS Competency #10*

On the wall of a classroom: "Always remember, your fathers never sold this land" is the caption on a poster showing an Indian face peering from behind the faces of Washington, Lincoln, Jefferson, and Theodore Roosevelt. Seen on the wall of another classroom: a display called "North American Indians," divided up by the continent's major Indian groups, with pictures and text associated with each group; to the right of the door—a book cover of *Black Elk Speaks,* a picture of Black Elk, and a poster of an Indian with arms reaching up to the sky; on another wall—a newspaper page devoted to the fetal alcohol syndrome that was written on the occasion of the television rendition of Michael Dorris's book, *The Broken Cord* (1989). On the wall of a bathroom stall: "San Juan rules the Northern Pueblos."

Some optional subjects with full Indian content that students can enroll in are silver work, drawing, Native American literature, and drumming. To begin the drumming class, the teacher, also a Pueblo musician, bends down on his left knee, invoking the Great Spirit. He asks for strength, gentle words, kindness, and more. He continues thereafter to pray in English. The class contains six boys and two girls. The girls sing but do not join the boys in their drumming accompaniment. Their parents believe it is improper for girls to drum, a decision the teacher feels is a parental prerogative. He explains to the students that the songs they sing are not associated with any tribe, hoping thereby to offend no one. At the same time that the drumming class meets, another teacher in a Native American literature class is teaching six students how to apply simile, metaphor, and symbolism to a story by Leslie Marmon Silko (Laguna Pueblo), and to others found in Geary Hobson's edited book *The Remembered Earth* (1979).

The intention and reality of integrating Indian content with a course's standard subject matter is less obvious in some places. In accounting, for example, the teacher indicates on a form called "Curricula Coursework Plans" that his integration involves study skills ("awareness of community computer accounting and impact on Indian culture"); higher order thinking skills ("compare and contrast computer accounting in Indian and non-Indian settings"); and Indian perspective ("small group discussion on how cultural values may change as more computers are introduced into the Indian communities"). On a similar form, the computer graphics teacher lists among his five goals that "the students will learn to construct complex Native American geometric designs and shapes for use with weavings, jewelry, and ceramic paintings." Integration, though not farfetched, is not easily accomplished in such subjects.

For the most part, it is not easy in mathematics either. In one class, the teacher does not so much integrate as tack on, telling a story at the end of the lesson about a needy single Indian mother with two children, who comes upon an anthill out of which grow flowers, berries, and beads, the gifts of a man who responded to her prayers for help. The teacher tells the students that they should always be "in a state of thankfulness for such beings" as this man.

English and social studies offer more fertile possibilities for integration, and the teachers capitalize on these possibilities, especially in writing assignments of all types. So it is that in one English class a student writes a letter to Supreme Court Justice David Souter in order to protest the Lyng vs. Northwest Indian Cemetery Protection Decision. "My religion," the student writes, "is the Catholic and my own secret culture that my ancestors have handed down. . . . Our religion tells us to respect the land that our Great Spirit has given to us. . . . It is sacred to us. . . . The Constitution is supposed to guarantee our freedom of religion. I feel that this law violates all Indian Religion Rights."

In another English class, a student writes an essay called "500 Years of Life and Death" that argues for not celebrating Columbus Day: "It is like people are celebrating the killing of many natives and the conqueror of them. . . . The question is, how did he discover America when so many people were already living there? Think about it and decide if it is right to celebrate Columbus." Another student writing on the same topic concludes his essay, "But the Indian is a very strong race and can not lose their religion. . . . We have lasted this long and I think that should be celebrated. Celebrating Columbus Day is like celebrating the day of the Manson murders."

The civics teacher seems especially attuned to integration. He begins his class with a call for the news, hoping that this will encourage students to read, watch, or listen to the news. One day he informs the class of the forthcoming feast days at Acoma and Isleta. He asks for raised hands of those who are from these Pueblos. One girl raises her hand. "Will you dance?" he asks her. She will not, but the teacher makes no pronouncements about this. Students know that as a traditional person he believes in participation.

On the civics room blackboard the teacher has written: "Class home-work—write 5 questions to ask Governor Dasheno on Wednesday," when he will speak to the class. "Today—discuss tribal governors according to the 9/11/91 handout," which is labeled "Tribal Government Who's Who?" Students must learn the names of the governors of the 19 tribes, and of the presidents of the Mescalero Apache, Jicarilla Apache, and Navajo Nation. One week later, students received a review sheet to help them prepare for the next day's test. Under "Tribal Government," the teacher had advised the students to know "three of the thirteen powers a sovereign nation" can have, the type of govern-ment the Iroquois had (students received another handout that identified the Iroquois as the "Real Founding Fathers of the U. S. Constitution"), and which Pueblos have a constitution.

Understanding the appeal of rap songs to their students, creative teachers across the country invite students to compose lyrics in this form, using content that fits their class's subject matter. Students at Indian High School are not to be outdone. In preparation for a forthcoming Academic Fair, four history students have written:

Today we are told to forget the past time
When our culture was in its greatest prime.
Still we don't listen to what they say,
because our culture will forever stay.
Some tribes have already lost.
Now without their old culture they have to pay the cost.
Now we must keep up the fight.
If we don't we must fade out of sight.

Another group has written:

The Natives today have become modernized
and through the white man's world have
Americanized.
Some tribal cultures continue to exist
Despite the Americanization the Natives resist.
As natives of the US of A we survived 500
years of prey.

A history teacher shows a video, "Surviving Columbus." "Pueblo life before contact was mostly spiritual," intones the narrator. "Pueblo people are tenacious and flexible. Before the Spanish invasion, they were successful and peaceful. There were one hundred Pueblos." A scene accompanied by the sound of rhythmic bells and singing encourages students to move and stomp to the beat, as do their elders at ceremonial events when they sit along the sidelines of their Pueblo's plaza watching the dance before them.

What I have described above does not go on all the time; students are not engaged in dense and invariably absorbing Indianizing experiences. Attending Indian High School will not discourage culturally committed students and will not predictably change the minds of culturally uncommitted students. Students on the commitment margin will have peer models available in each direction.

At Indian High School, elements of Indian culture are blended, mixed, fused—many terms can be used to reflect the nature of the integration of Indian and non-Indian components in the regular school program—to an extent that far surpasses the integration in other schools Pueblo students are apt to attend, and to an extent beyond that in most schools other distinctive minority groups attend. The result is a school whose outside-world thrust is moderated by traditional knowledge and culture, whose flavor is never fully non-Indian, whose intentions cannot be seen as hostile to Indian culture or Indian people, and whose impact may well invigorate, not just reinforce, traditional commitments. Indian High School is a contact situation where Indian people meet non-Indian culture, one that has been constructed and Indianized to the extent that its educators can manage to do so, given the religious and linguistic constraints they must respect.

As theocracies, Pueblo tribal communities are shaped by religion. They extend to Indian High School their concern for survival not only in nontraditional terms, but also in traditional terms; the school's dual charge responds to its students' obligation to learn to live in two worlds. Ironically, what the school does in the name of creating an Indian school may, broadly speaking, originate in Pueblo culture, but it most definitely is not a religious school. It differs from other religious schools—such as Catholic, Lutheran, Jewish—that can freely infuse the school experience with religious doctrine. Indian High School and religious schools may speak the same language of integration, but Pueblo restrictions prevent Indian High School from being similarly shaped by religion. It remains, in essence, a school of the outside world, of the dominant whiteman's society.

Eight pictures hang on the wall of Indian High School's career office. Together they tell the story about picking a career—"the sky is the limit"—and staying attached to one's Indian community. The first picture contains the message, "Help us continue to be together. Find your working career that we may stay together." In short, while reaching for the career sky, keep your feet squarely planted on the good earth of your Pueblo. The seventh picture portrays a Pueblo setting and two figures—a male holding books, a female holding a notebook—each connected to the Pueblo by a line. The accompanying message reads, "Part of my life includes my work." That is, one's career is a part of life; one's Pueblo is the rest. The eighth picture shows a young man and an old man, with this message: "We are together you and I," meaning, read your books, build a career, but remember your elders and their wisdom, and your place in the continuity of culture.

These pictures depict a Pueblo ideal that builds upon elements of both worlds. Realizing this ideal is, perhaps, their ultimate challenge.

3

"Preserving What We Love and Cherish": Pueblo Ideals

I prayed for direction from the Clay Mother, and slowly the information began to come...
I also asked for the help of my great-grandmother and my great-aunts, who were all potters.
And I still ask their guidance today.

—Lonnie Vigil, Nambe Potter

INTRODUCTION

New Mexico's combined group of Pueblo, Apache, and Navajo Indians com-
prises 130,000 people, or 12% of the state population. Pueblo tribal officials
dispute these and other figures from the Bureau of the Census (1992) as
underestimations.[1] In absolute numbers, it is the fourth largest Indian state,
behind California (200,000), Oklahoma (170,000), and Arizona (153,000); in
percentage, it is the largest. Two thirds of the nation's nearly 2,000,000 Indians
live west of the Mississippi River; about 25% live on reservations. Were
numbers alone the basis for salience in official or popular awareness, Indians
might well be forgotten, but as Karen Swisher, director of the Center for
American Indian Education at Arizona State University, reminds us, "We have
a special relationship with the people of this country and we shouldn't be
forgotten" (cited in O'Brien n.d.:26).

Pueblo Indians do have a special relationship with the other peoples of New
Mexico. Their political, economic, and cultural presence places them promi-
nently in local and state affairs. Their approximately 30,000 reservation mem-

---

[1]What also is disputed is what personal circumstances the tribes designate as the basis for being
accepted as a tribal member. This formal procedure may be in conflict with a person's self-iden-
tification as an Indian who belongs to a certain tribe.

bers are dispersed among the 19 tribes. They live on tribal land that stretches almost continuously along the Rio Grande from north of Taos to south of Albuquerque, and then west along I-40 from Albuquerque to the Arizona border. As Table 3.1 shows, the Zuni have the largest reservation-based population. At least another 20 percent or more of each tribe live off their reservations (Bodine 1972:225), some of them permanent residents in urban areas, some living off their reservations indefinitely as they find jobs and make homes elsewhere both inside and outside New Mexico. The Pueblo presence is observable on the special occasions of public dances and markets, in the form of artistic products always on sale throughout the state, in regular newspaper coverage, and by means of highway signs designating the approach to a reservation.

Pueblo life is touched by the work of many external organizations, but it is most definitely focussed within each tribal reservation. Here are found the adobe homes and plazas and holy places, both native and Catholic, where the routine and special activities of Pueblo life are played out. The reservation communities are set within vistas of mountain, sky, and land devoted to agriculture and grazing animals. They contain buildings for administration and recreation, and often an elementary school, whose graduates have the choice thereafter to attend a local public school or Indian High School. Dirt roads crisscross the settlements. Cars, people, and dogs stir up the dust year-long, save during the winter months when snow may cover the ground, or when the rain has come to bless this people who dance it into existence. Pueblo villages, located within expanses of land away from towns and main highways, suggest tranquility, remoteness, even isolation. The roads leading out of their communities, however, are also the roads leading in; they could not be isolated if they chose to be. Like Indian High School, the reservations are inevitably, inexorably attached to the mainland of Anglo society.

The legal status of reservations (a complex issue beyond the scope of my study; see Sando [1992], especially chapter 4) places each tribe in continual engagement with one or another level of federal, state, and local government. If tribal leaders must be prepared to engage in political dealings with all levels of government, individual Indians almost invariably must be engaged in economic dealings. The once-dominant agricultural basis of Pueblo life has been replaced by jobs outside the reservations. To be sure, livestock and cultivation still engage some families, and many more plant relatively modest amounts of corn and perhaps other crops, but farming is no longer the economic mainstay for most families. Outside jobs in non-Indian shops, businesses, factories, and offices demand educational credentials as the ticket to employment, plus competence in English and social interactional skills for getting and keeping a job. Even those whose entrepreneurial work focuses on art—pottery, painting,

TABLE 3.1

Reservation-Based Population of the Pueblo Tribes, 1990

Tribe	Population
Acoma	2,551
Cochiti	666
Isleta	2,699
Jemez	1,738
Laguna	3,634
Nambe	329
Picuris	147
Pojaque	177
Sandia	358
San Felipe	1,859
San Ildefonso	347
San Juan	1,276
Santa Ana	481
Santa Clara	1,246
Santo Domingo	2,947
Taos	1,212
Tesuque	232
Zia	637
Zuni	7,073
Total	29,609

Note. These figures are taken from the *Indian High School Annual Report*, 1990. See Bodine (1972) for tribal population data for 1942, 1950, 1964, and 1968.

jewelry, beadwork—must relate to non-Indian markets in which these competencies and skills are requisite.

The tribes themselves must be economically viable. In the past, outsiders exploited the natural resources of tribal land. Today, in quest of economic self-sufficiency, tribal initiatives include camping facilities, gas stations, shops, casinos, hotels, and factories. Their success requires people with sophisticated administrative, financial, planning, and legal skills. As prominent as each tribe's traditional religious leaders are (in some tribes, these leaders choose the people who will manage their secular affairs), the demands of tribal survival require placing people in positions of power who are accomplished in non-Indian language, knowledge, and skills.

Take the case of land, a matter of historic despair and contemporary unease. Pueblo tribes are determined not only to stem further loss of land, but also to regain by purchase and litigation former tribal lands occupied by non-Indians. Therefore, tribal leaders encourage the acquisition of academic credentials. They would like to have their own people in the role of legal counsel negotiating land issues with government lawyers, and end their dependence on non-Pueblo professionals. Dealing with land issues and other unavoidable issues of non-Indian life demands not just contact with the outside world, but also acquiring the skills and talents of that world. As another case, take that of tribal government itself. Each tribe has a governor who usually serves a 1-year term, and heads a group of officials that manages the tribe's secular affairs. It is useful if governors can speak their tribal language; it is essential that they speak English.

Land is a mythic, sacralized good in traditional Pueblo culture. Several writers place its significance in perspective:

N. Scott Momaday ... reached to the remembrance of his childhood at Jemez, New Mexico. "I existed in that landscape," he wrote ... , "and then my existence was indivisible with it." [Vizenor 1994:10]

Secure in the possession of their lands, the Pueblo Indians are safe and virtually independent; without their lands they would meet quick and utter ruin. [White 1942:73]

The fight for land and water is a struggle for survival of the Pueblo people ... *That these people shall endure upon the earth* is all the Pueblos want. [Sando 1992:131–2]

Pueblo land is not real estate, a mere commodity, a marketable item like cars and refrigerators available for buying, selling, and trading. It is, rather, the foundation of sovereignty and culture, just as religion is the substance of community, culture, and personal identity. Together, land, religion, and the structures of governance establish each tribal community as a theocracy (see Ball 1990:137; Goldfrank 1952:74; Hawley 1937:514; Gutiérrez 1991:22). One Pueblo man explained: "When I say religious, there are a lot of things that follow and I can't really break it down for you. To me, that means everything, the whole major core of a Native American, belonging to your tribe and the community." Traditional Indian religion encompasses tribal communities, notwithstanding that most Pueblo people also are Catholic.[2] Pueblo people acknowledge the role of the spirits in hunting, working with clay, opening and closing meetings, eating—indeed, in all human activity. "Life at Jemez," observes Ball, "is ordered by a ceremonial cycle more religious than secular in orientation" (1990:137).

The *kiva* is the center for formal socialization in the Pueblo community (see Horgan 1970; Fergusson 1931; Smith 1990; and Gutiérrez 1991). Each tribe has one or more *kivas*. Typically, these are round buildings entered via a ladder or steps that lead up to an opening on the roof, and then down into a large, windowless space. The *kiva* is a sacred center, closed to all non-Indian outsiders, a place of instruction and preparation for ritual practice. Young and old Pueblo people engage in, and are engaged by, both *kiva* and school instruction, with all that each connotes for how to live one's life. What each connotes is also the basis for what is certain and uncertain for Pueblo communities as communities, and for Pueblo people as individuals.

On the one hand, what occurs in school is without mystery, its ends and means fully public, its conduct the stuff of open discussion and debate. If the opportunities schools provide are not self-evident or accessible equally to everyone, it is not because of anything intentionally obscure or closed about the process of schooling. On the other hand, the ends and means of what occurs in the *kiva* and in most of Pueblo religious life are purposely hidden from non-Pueblo people. They are hidden by habits of secrecy (see Smith 1990:116–9; Walker 1972:22; Scheper-Hughes 1987:72–3) that were forged in the face of Spanish accusations of Pueblo paganism and objectionable practice. The results of such accusations are evident in Governor Juan Ignacio Flores Mogollón's 1714 memorandum: "I have had word that at the pueblo of Pecos [now extinct except as a monument] a partially subterranean room ... has been built ... inasmuch as there are in addition to this one others in said pueblo, I order the alcalde mayor to go immediately and ascertain if it is true. If it is, he will make them destroy and demolish it immediately" (Kessell 1979:309).

---

[2]Each reservation has a Catholic church; some reservations allow only Catholic churches to operate on tribal land. Their experience with fundamentalist churches has been negative because the latter reject traditional Pueblo religion in a way that the Catholic church does not. (See Fox 1973:277–8.)

Mogollón's objections had been preceded in the 1670s by the Franciscan missionaries' attack on certain types of dancers as "heathen idols" (Spicer 1972:185) that should be suppressed.

Although Pueblo religious procedure went underground partly in reaction to Spanish intolerance (where, for the most part, it remains today), it is also true that religious knowledge was never meant to be open, even within the Pueblo community. As summarized by Joseph Suina (Cochiti), "The single motive for withholding information is that the criteria for knowledge have not been attained" (1991:18). This information is most emphatically denied to curious tourists and inquiring scholars. Anthropologist Elsie Clews Parsons dedicated a 1936 paper she wrote "To my best [Indian] friend in Taos ... who told me nothing about the pueblo, and who never will tell any white person anything his people would not have him tell, which is nothing" (quoted in Smith 1990:119). Every Pueblo youngster learns that "what goes on in the *kiva* stays in the *kiva*." Parents may send their young children to school with a clear reminder: "You know, your teachers may not understand that they shouldn't ask you certain questions. Just say, 'I'm sorry, I can't talk about that.'"

PUEBLO IDEALS

"From early childhood we learn the traditional ways of Indian life," observes an older Pueblo man. His grandmother taught him to "be a strong believer in our Indian way." This way, varied in its particulars among the Pueblo tribes, builds upon a core of common beliefs and practices that are rooted in Pueblo ideals.[3] Within each tribe, the core is basically uncontested; no other ideals prevail. Pueblo ideals have reality in Pueblo life as ideals, recognized as such, highly valued, but by no means a picture of the daily actuality of Pueblo communities or individuals. They most definitely function the way ideals do and should, as a group's best sense of what it aspires to be. I do not see these ideals as a romanticized version of Pueblo life. Unsurprisingly, Pueblo ideals can be contested, as John Bennett wrote in his 1946 article, "The Interpretations of Pueblo Culture."

That Pueblo ideals have continuing currency in the life of the tribes was confirmed by a Pueblo teacher: "The ideal is something to strive for, yes, and it is something that is always changing, too. I mean, I think, there is an element

---

[3]Harrod (1995:19–30) elaborates on the dual function of tribal core ideals as the basis of both continuity and response to change, establishing a point of departure and a point of return, the dynamic terms of tribal order. For more on Pueblo cultural ideals and practice see Suina and Smolkin (1994).

of permanency, but things around it are always changing. I think the stronger that permanent part is, the stronger the community is, and the stronger it will be against change." The teacher captures one potentially paradoxical outcome of sustaining tradition and accommodating to social change: the stronger the core, the stronger the community; but the stronger the core and the community, the better it can resist change; and the better it can resist change, the more certainly it may resist learning how to accommodate change.

The core is not fully incorporated into the structures of belief and behavior of all Pueblo members, notwithstanding its status as ideal. Individual Indians do accept other beliefs, follow other practices. The ideals as ideals are essentially intact, even though challenged by the immense alternatives of the outside world that sweep like waves onto the shores of Pueblo communities. Thus alternatives, like the core itself, are facts of Pueblo life, but not ideal facts. Alternatives lack the authenticity that time and incorporation into sacred tradition afford to Pueblo ideals.

Because the core prevails as the Pueblo ideal, it has an aura of certainty and authority. We see these qualities in the taunting words of an elderly Hopi[4] man: "If I raise a family, clothe and feed them well, do my ceremonial duties faithfully, I have succeeded—what do you call success?" (Eggan 1976:153). We see them also in the words of Simon Ortiz, as he reflects on his parents' emphasis on acquiring traditional knowledge. Without such knowledge, says Ortiz, he could not be "fulfilled personally and on behalf of his community." The stories instructing him "were common knowledge of act, event, and behavior.... It was the stories and songs which provided the knowledge that I saw woven into the intricate web that was my Acoma life" (Ortiz 1987:189). Identifying learning as "common knowledge" that is necessary for being "fulfilled personally" stamps it with the hallmark of singular consequence, not merely one among a lineup of choices, like the many offerings on a cafeteria counter.

Most fundamentally, I mean to indicate by this overview of Pueblo culture that Pueblo people live in communities that embody a distinct, complete, intact way of life. To be sure, these communities are decidedly not the places of pre-European contact, not even the places of 25 years ago. Their ways are neither purely distinct, fully complete, nor wholly intact. But they suffice in each of these respects, and the resulting community is a place and people apart.

"There is no salvation in tribal religion," says Vine Deloria Jr., "apart from continuance of the tribe itself.... It is ... a covenant with a particular god and a particular community" (quoted in Highwater 1981:169). In its application to

---

[4]Most often, Hopi Indians are listed as a Pueblo tribe but my references from Indian High School confine their list to the 19 Pueblo tribes that are in New Mexico.

the Pueblos or any other tribe, this notion of Deloria's entails salvation in particular terms that tribes themselves define. At the center of the terms for Pueblo tribes is harmony and balance, and what this means for the behavior of its members: keeping people and things in harmonious relationship depends on the knowledge, ability, and willingness of members to behave appropriately and to feel appropriately. A Pueblo ninth grader wrote in an essay that his "grandma would tell my dad ... 'that your pottery will talk to you ... and in order to have a good piece of pottery your life has to be balanced. If your life is not balanced, your pottery will resemble how your life is.'"

Edward Dozier, anthropologist and Santa Clara Pueblo tribesman, wrote of "man and the universe ... conceived to be in a kind of balance" (1956:494), of the "harmonious balance of the universe," and of Pueblo people "working together with harmonious feeling toward all things in the universe" (1956:495). Maintaining harmony means that unlike the American mainstream that values individuality or "standing out," Pueblos endorse "standing in," so that one becomes "so identified with the group that one's individuality is not noticed" (Weisz et al., quoted by Sampson 1985:1204). By standing in, Sampson continues, people seek "to fit into the ongoing scheme of things through ... a person system designed to minimize self-other distinctions" (1985:1205).

From Pueblo conceptions of harmony and balance, of fitting in, not standing out, follow much that underlies Pueblo behavior. Children learn that a sense of responsibility to their tribal group must pervade their lives if the tribe's well-being is to be sustained. There is, accordingly, a tension between obligations to self, family, and group that is not readily resolved when enticements to personal opportunity from the outside world confront the imperatives of community obligations. This tension arises from the intersection of a non-Indian world that emphasizes the individual with an Indian world whose ideal is to emphasize the group. For a study conducted many years ago, researcher Anne Smith interviewed Pueblo people. One student told her: "When any Pueblo Indian is asked questions about himself as an individual, the thing that pops into my mind is always 'group.' To me, the word individual still does not exist" (Smith 1966:83). Emphasis on the group or "the common good" (Siegel 1952:137) is another standard of Pueblo life that distinguishes it from most other American groups—the obligation to put your tribe before yourself and to accept leadership responsibility when tribal officials offer it to you. Serving the common good is a core value.

Within the Pueblo value of "standing in," individuals do indeed excel in traditional ways. Pueblo communities recognize and appreciate excellence in leaders, orators, dancers, singers, artists, cooks, storytellers, and the like. Excelling, however, is framed by a sense of egalitarianism that invites one not to strut or trumpet one's talents and successes. One must manage the trick of simultaneously being outstanding or successful in some way and not calling attention to oneself, except as one's performance may do so. The fine potter's wares speak for themselves; the potter's behavior must not be perceived as doing so. In addition, talented people pay homage to their group by their uncoerced teaching of others, by their sharing of talents, so that others may learn from them (Romero 1992).

Correct behavior about what one does conforms with the commitment to harmony. This includes behaving in a noncompetitive way. One means not to do better than others, even though one does; seeking to outdo others is an unbalancing act, whereas fully doing one's best is not. Striving in the sense of doing well, even outstandingly well, as one is able to, is acceptable. Taking life as it comes, accepting and being happy with one's lot, is valued. It comes down to being content with who one is, as destiny dictates, and not trying to be who one is not. Such behavior contrasts with the assertiveness Pueblos see as typical of the non-Indian world.

Furthermore, one should not expect to be singled out by praise and commendation. The ideal is to manage recognizing things done well without praising the individual in unseemly ways that exalt the person. The ideal is to create honor rolls of the heart, not of neon signs and billboards. Pueblo people risk violating community norms when the outside world acknowledges their achievements, notwithstanding that non-Indians are doing the praising. The norms of appropriateness are not suspended because the singling out occurs beyond tribal boundaries. A Pueblo woman remarks, "If I get too visible, people will start gossiping about me and bring me down to earth. There's a tendency in Pueblo culture to try and make sure that everybody is kind of at the same level."

The stress on harmony includes observing the details of an act, a performance, an event. "Harmonizing all the particulars" is how one person stated this point. "Observing the details," "not taking shortcuts" in preparations for ceremonial activities, is important. Pueblos contrast their emphasis on following the guidelines of conduct in an exacting manner with the presumed non-Indian emphasis on straight-line, time-conscious conduct rooted in an ethic of getting things done fast and efficiently. As one woman said of traditional conduct, "You do exactly as it is laid out for you to do," a reference to cooking, costuming, dancing, all activities, whatever they may be.

Showing respect to elders, tribal officers, and religious leaders is a way of fitting in to keep the community in harmony. Those who show respect get respect in return, in the sense of being listened to and supported. Pueblo youth probably hear more about showing respect than any other core concept: "What I learned from my parents and my grandparents was to respect everything. You are a human being, you are on this earth. Everything on this planet is supposed to be respected. That way you live in balance with nature, and that will make you whole."

Becoming whole is the personal reward for acquiring cultural knowledge and thereby doing right, fitting in, showing respect, and living a balanced life. Practically speaking, one is never completely whole; one is, rather, always in the process of becoming whole. Wholeness is an abstract, subjective state of fulfillment that is more readily spoken of in the negative: for example, one is not fulfilled if one does not pray, does not work with a good heart, does not contribute to communal occasions. Doing these things promotes the fulfillment of wholeness, but it does not guarantee it. Says a Pueblo man, "You can't become whole without the knowledge to do so," and you are always dependent on those who possess the knowledge to teach you, when they think you are ready. Because knowledge of wholeness gradually unfolds, youth and older people alike are only partially informed: "It's like a puzzle, putting a puzzle together. Once you put all that puzzle together, I guess by the time you're old, that's when you're probably whole. Or maybe you're not whole when you're still here on earth."

At some of the most religiously conservative[5] Pueblos, fluency in one's vernacular language—a version of Keresan (usually referred to as "Keres") spoken in the Southern Pueblos, or Tanoan (usually referred to as "Tewa" or "Tiwa") spoken in the Northern Pueblos—may be deemed a necessary condition for attaining wholeness. Pueblo young and old are forthrightly clear about the relationship between their vernacular and maintaining their tribe's religious orthodoxy. Though religion cannot be fully practiced without the vernacular, those who do not know it may wholeheartedly join in the spirit of the occasion. To the contrary, Pueblo religious leaders must be competent in their tribal language, as priests must be in Latin and rabbis in Hebrew, but even more so. The Pueblos do not have nonvernacular written or spoken versions of their religious expression to draw upon. There is resistance to developing an orthography for Pueblo languages, given the intimate relationship between Pueblo language and religion. Furthermore, because their language has survived forever by oral transmission, there is a powerful sentiment that, as an educator expressed it, "Writing and reading are whiteman's tools. Writing and reading are not our way."[6]

Forms of the Indian languages vary, ranging from the polish, sophistication, and depth required for complex religious activity to the technical capability useful for transacting tribal business and governance, to the basic, everyday

---

[5]Pueblo members may disagree among themselves about which Pueblo individuals are more or less conservative. "Conservative" is not a pejorative term, and it is a relative matter. A woman describes herself: "I consider myself traditional, but, then, someone else from, say, San Felipe, can look at me and say I'm not really traditional in their terms."

[6]See Fox (1973:261–6) for a useful discussion of language usage at Cochiti Pueblo in the recent past that can be extended to other Pueblos as well.

language of family and routine social contact. Learning the most sophisticated form of the language is open or closed to people as they are eligible to acquire cultural knowledge and assume tribal responsibility. Therefore, some vocabulary and thought forever will be closed to those who fail to satisfy the conditions for knowing.

Grandparents, the keepers of language and tradition, adapt their linguistic practice to the varied circumstances of their lives. "My children's grandma will tell them what she wants done or make requests of them in Tewa. They respond in English. Her youngest daughter is about 19 and from her on up when she's angry or lecturing, whatever, she'll do it in Indian. For the younger ones, she'll kind of talk in both, like she'll say what she wants in Indian, then she'll repeat it in English." It is not certain that this grandmother's grandchildren will learn, let alone master, some form of the vernacular. What is more certain is that their lives will at least be touched by circumstances that demand a need to know it. Pueblo elders contend that if you want to make a request to religious leaders, you cannot do it in the language of everyday speech, let alone in English. Moreover, these religious leaders cannot address the spirits in any but the sophisticated form of language suitable for religious expression. Elders claim that only the vernacular can communicate and explain the nature of their traditional activities; English will not do.

Pueblo people hear the intentionally repeated message of fitting in, showing respect, and learning their language. Within their tribal communities, another often-heard message everyone learns is the nature and necessity of participation. Forms of participation vary by gender and age. Elders stress bringing children as young as two or three to ceremonial and domestic activity so that they can be involved, see how things are done, and hear the language that accompanies a particular activity.

Both boys and girls are taught that to be a proper community member is to participate. This obligation is not set aside because of one's education or work, or where one lives. A high school senior girl, college-bound, captures the ideal sense of participation:

> I will participate the way I was taught. I started off young helping at things like dances, and even when I go off to college and come back I know there will be people to teach me. So I don't think I will change in any way. Unless it is really impossible, I will be home [for ceremonial events]. When you come to traditional ceremonial things, all the ladies don't just take responsibility for their own family, they take responsibility for the whole tribe.

A Pueblo woman powerfully communicates the rewards of participation that sustain her and motivate her to teach her children its virtues:

When we participate and have our heart in it, there is a peace of mind. You can lose yourself. God, it is so beautiful. You just forget about, like, "Is the laundry done? Are the bills paid? Do I have to go to work?" Everything is so good and wonderful! No wonder our grandparents felt so good. That is why they wanted this [their tradition] to continue, and that is when you get the yearning of saying, "I want my kids to have this."

Secular community work, usually the annual cleaning of the reservation's water-carrying ditches, is expected of adult males; if they do not participate, they are fined. Doing such work is a condition for remaining on the Pueblo, by which fact, and others,[7] we learn that residence at a Pueblo is not fully a personal choice. Living in the family house on land the family long has occupied does not ensure the right to remain there if one violates tribal norms. However, most people live as community members within a network of expectations that are taught, modeled, and rewarded. A man explained, "You can't tell another person how it feels, but there is such a joy that you get after you prepare and participate."

Aside from the obligatory work, other types of participation carry the force of strong expectation, but, ultimately, they are voluntary. If one lives far away from the Pueblo, one should try to return at least once a year for ceremonial activity; if one lives off-reservation but nearby, more frequent returning is possible and expected. Moreover, in the course of acquiring one's non-Indian educational credentials, one learns that the fruits of one's education are supposed to benefit the tribe.

Older Pueblo adults are more certainly knowledgeable about and responsive to the tribal ideal of participation. Adolescents, particularly those who attend boarding schools, could, possibly, be less well-informed and committed. Their words suggest otherwise. Almost without exception, students verify the importance of participation in their tribe's extensive ceremonial round, but also its voluntary nature. It is their decision, and their parents accept it as their decision, notwithstanding parental preference that they do participate, and their disappointment if they do not. Grandparents and other elders may feel less permissive about participation, believing that it is not best to give young people so free a choice. They may be upset if their grandchildren do not participate, because, as one girl said concisely, but with a volume of meaning, "My grandmother really believes in her tradition." Moreover, grandparents are sensitive, knowing that if family members do not participate, others will wonder what is going on in

---

[7]As several interviewees explained, born-again Christian Pueblo members on some reservations may be asked to leave because of the exclusivist outlook of their religious doctrine. Being born-again precludes their participation in ceremonial activity in a way that Catholicism does not.

the family and question how it raises its children. The student's sense of choice, however actually free, derives from a tribal belief that forced participation does not lead to the pure mind and heart that is the right condition for participation.

Students explain their participation by communal reasons, saying that participation is necessary to "keep your culture alive" and by personal reasons, saying, "It just makes you feel good." One young man expressed the point with particular eloquence: "The feast days are like celebrating, almost like a birthday. You're there and you're dancing and you're helping. Within my tribe, it's like you get renewed during that day. It's like a rebirth. You can start again."[8] For such people, the apparent hardships of dancing—long hours in the heat or cold, continuous physical exertion, fasting—dissipate from the joy they experience. The young people overcome the hardships, such as they are, having been assured that this will happen. An adult explained: "Even though they're kids, they know they're proud of themselves. They're partners in everything.... A lot of time they tell some of the younger kids that want to take part, 'You're gonna get tired, you're gonna get sleepy.' So it's almost like a challenge: 'I'm ready. I'm ready.'" Students know that it is the norm to participate; they see that it also is the norm not to participate. While some tribal members reside at their Pueblo, they are, at best, peripheral members, doing what they must to be allowed to stay, and little more.

Religious positions at all Pueblos are attained by invitation from a tribe's religious leadership. This is mostly true as well for the secular administrative positions of governor, lieutenant governor, and others that compose the tribal council; in several Pueblos, these positions are elective. The request to serve is an honor. It can come at any time in an adult's, usually a man's, life, regardless of where he is living or what he is doing. The person's personal circumstances—in the middle of an educational program, in a good job with unsympathetic bosses who will not grant a leave with the right to return, in a career in progress that will be halted by leaving, in a well-paying job that supports a substantial standard of living—do not generally stop tribal leaders from making the request. For full-time, 1-year appointments, things work best when the person can get a leave of absence from his job, with the right to return. For full-time, life-long appointments, thought to be one's destiny, one's life is completely reoriented. In both cases, the appointee's family must become allies

---

[8]Mostly, I take on face value what the students told me. At the time of our interviews, I had been at Indian High School for months and knew the students fairly well. I told them that I wanted to learn no more than what they really knew, believed, and felt. Talking with them over a period of months led, I believe, to achieving reasonably straightforward expression. Still, it strikes me that in this and some other cases students might have presented a true but possibly heightened version of their aspirations and behavior. This observation also applies to adults.

in facilitating the honored person's removal from his usual activities, enduring disruptions in recognition of their family member's fulfillment of his responsibility.

A man who serves his tribe in a musical capacity captures some of the special feelings that accompany his role. It is a role, like several others, that allows a man to keep his outside-world occupation, but requires him at frequent intervals to join his talent to ceremonial activity. "You have to leave work and go home and get prepared for that evening. It's sitting there and singing songs, listening to songs. It's very hard physically. Mentally, it's very strengthening. When you get home, you're tired, but you have that fulfillment. Hey, you know, we're getting prepared for something that's wonderful."

Being singled out to serve carries both honor and costs. It is difficult indeed to experience the disruption, for a year or a lifetime, of plans, progress, and opportunities in one's work in the outside world. Surely, some invitees have refused the honor to serve; no one I spoke with acknowledged knowing any. "I don't know of anyone personally, in the past or now, saying no to his appointment. At any Pueblo, it's all males and they're appointed by their religious leaders. No one has said no and I wouldn't want to be the first. I have no idea of just what would happen to the whole tribe or even to the individual himself. He might even get disenrolled from the tribe." These words convey the relationship between individual behavior and tribal well-being. The words of another man, a member of a more religiously conservative Pueblo, describe the relationship between accepting responsibility and the consequences of personal choice. A Pueblo man

knows he is going to get that call anytime. He could say no, but [if he does] he is going to give up all that he worked for, where he came from, who he is, what he is. He is going to give all that up because the tribe will probably tell him, "You need to move away. We gave you all this, you lived on our land, we helped you grow, and now you are saying no. You can now move away." You are involved with this company or corporation. They [tribal officials] see your leadership skills. That is what we call the two-worlds conflict. They look at you and want you here on this [the Pueblo's] side. You don't have choices. They make them for you.

Pueblo men and women are encouraged to develop talents that derive from both their Indian and non-Indian worlds, but it is expected that all talents, whatever their origin, should, if requested, be placed at the service of the tribe. In matters of ceremony and other occasions for participation, Indians who claim to be too busy with their outside jobs may be accused of acting white. The ideal is to make the sacrifices, to put one's tribal community first: being too busy is a whiteman's excuse.

Some teaching of cultural knowledge is formalized in the roles of persons who serve the entire tribe; other instruction falls, by custom, to family elders, most usually to a grandparent, but lacking a grandparent, to godparents, aunts or uncles, less typically to parents. Teaching within the family, teaching extended over time, teaching to be taken seriously, teaching performed by respected persons, teaching meant both for children and for their parents—all this is customary. Children are taught to respond most seriously to their grandparents. Parents advise their children, "Listen to the elders, take in all that is said to you, have a lot of respect, and listen."

In many cultures, grandparents have been central figures in socializing the young, their wisdom and experience treasured because they could be found nowhere else. Respecting one's elders came naturally. This circumstance still prevails within Pueblo communities, however much eroded here and there by social change. Anthropologist Nancy Scheper-Hughes testifies to the centrality of the grandparent when she quotes a bereaved adolescent boy: "I miss my grandfather. I don't know how to be a Pueblo without him." She continues with further reference to the singularity of the grandparent: "The older generation of grandfathers can come to represent ... an almost unattainable standard of cultural integrity and purity" (1987:65). "Unlike you whites," a Pueblo woman explained to Scheper-Hughes, "we keep our grandparents with us until we die" (1987:67).

Other Pueblo adults and adolescents I interviewed reinforce this picture of grandparental importance. A woman speaks of her mother-in-law's role in her own life and the life of her children:

> When their grandmother comes, she demands a higher respect. It is just in her actions, how she treats them, her role in the family. They know that she is telling them something that they need to know. Sometimes she will lecture them about what is happening, how it used to be, and what they need to do. Grandparents also get mad at their own children, like me. They can come in and tell us what we are doing wrong. If something comes up that I don't understand, then I would ask her, and she's always willing to tell me what I need to know or what to do.

A student recalls words of her grandmother that reveal grandparental self-awareness of their place in Pueblo society. "As the days go by," her grandmother said, "my wisdom will be carried on by you and every one of my grandchildren. So when I am gone, the only part of me that will be gone is my body. I will live forever because of you." By these words, the grandmother implies that her "wisdom" is stamped with tradition's seal of approval, with authentication, therefore, for what is memorable to Pueblo people. She authoritatively conveys Pueblo ideals.

And another student speaks of her grandmothers, combining relish and nostalgia as she describes their contribution: "My grandma used to tell me these stories that my great-grandma told before. Great-grandma just died a year ago. She was one of those kind that never got out of the house. She was a pretty special person for everybody. She was our foundation. She stayed in the traditional way. I just wish it could be that way again."

This great-grandmother, and others like her, embodies Pueblo ideals that were shaped in times less complicated by dual-world challenges of the type that prevail today. As exemplars for young people, they can model and scold in the name of behaviors that come easier to them. The connection between grandparents and tradition? "I think it is like glue," said a woman who, as her parents' oldest child, lived with her grandparents until she was ready to enter high school. "If you don't have it, there isn't a way to be cohesive. My grandmother was the one who made a difference." Grandparents may carry an aura that lingers long after their death. They are thought of fondly, in terms that capture their special, and specialized, place. "I don't remember his [grandfather's] exact words, but I know they were how we sacredly concern ourselves with the people and the holy earth.... I know that his knowledge was vast ... and I listened as a boy should" (Ortiz 1987:189–90).

Indian High School students say that they, too, "listen as a boy should," at least at home. As boarding students they lack daily contact with their revered elders, but they seldom fail to visit their grandparents during their usual Friday afternoon to Sunday afternoon weekend at home. The students' visit—"the first thing I do is check on them"—is expected and welcomed by relatives who enjoy youthful company, ears, and working hands. "My grandpa always knows I will come by. I come on Friday." Along with cooking, cleaning, gathering wood, and doing whatever needs to be done, the students will hear stories about the past, get advice about their responsibilities as a man or woman, be taught how to pray, and be told what is right and wrong. If there's "something going on," an indirect reference to ceremonial activity, they are advised that they "better go over there and help," rehearing what Pueblo persons know: tribal well-being requires tribal members' participation.

In response to the teaching of their elders, students explained, learners are expected to listen, observe, and remember, expectations even more strongly endorsed in formal religious teaching sessions where personal pleasure or discomfort should not affect the behavior of the learner. Tribal leaders expect silence, patience, attention, and intention to learn. As regards sacred knowledge, learners can anticipate, when they have satisfied the criteria for knowing, that they will be told "more and more as you go along," though not generally by asking questions. Pueblo learners are socialized to understand that the outside world's emphasis on assertively seeking to know is not desirable in their tribal setting. They also know that they further the cause of their own learning by the quality of their demonstrated interest and sincerity in learning, appreciating all along the boundaries of knowledge—what they may not yet be taught, and what they must never share with unqualified others. Of all North American tribes, Pueblo Indians may take most seriously the learning and teaching of children and adults (Goldfrank 1952).

PUEBLO REMAINING

One day I received in my Indian High School mailbox a piece of lavender-colored paper. It was folded in half. On the outside flap was a picture of a seated Indian woman in traditional dress, her legs stretched before her on the ground. Her baby leaned against her, sitting between her legs. Inside was an invitation to a baby-shower potluck and a poem, its author unidentified:

> Whose voice I hear in the winds,
> And whose breath gives life to all the world,
> hear me! I am small and weak, I need your
> strength and wisdom....
> Make My Hands respect the things you have
> made and my ears sharp to hear your voice.
> Make Me Wise so that I may understand the
> things you have taught my people.
> Let Me Learn the lessons you have hidden
> in every leaf and rock....

This poem gives authority "to preserving what we love and cherish," as Indian High School's board president said on the occasion of the school's centennial celebration. "We've survived the worst of the assimilationist policies," he continued, "and the shocks we faced when we left the reservations ... What we have left, we'd like to keep."

What is left to keep is summarized by a Pueblo professional woman: "There's a different word for it in all the Pueblos, but it's a word that means, like, everything we are is tied up into one thing. Out of that comes the language, and out of that comes respect, and out of that comes who we are. When that gets broken down, like through families or kids not listening, then everybody loses something." What remains of the Pueblo culture's past of "eternal yesterdays" (Heilman 1977:232) is the basis for Pueblo people being able to say, as expressed by a non-Pueblo man, "I can walk confidently toward the future knowing full well that I can grasp whatever is out there because my own center

is secured" (Asante 1993:143). This is the ideal, the stars that guide the journeys
of Pueblo communities and Pueblo people.[9]

From the outside world comes the external dynamic of change in Pueblo
peoples' lives, the opportunity for material satisfaction, and for adventure in
the relative unknown. From the inside world are community and meaning, the
opportunity for certain other satisfactions, and for patterned adventures in the
known. Those who devote themselves to their culture may be rewarded: "You
feel you're whole. Every part of your life is fulfilled—your soul, your body,
your mind. I think it is kind of a total commitment, but a total fulfillment, too."
Thus is meaning expressed. More than this, says a Pueblo man, is "belonging
to and knowing that you are accepted as part of the community. To me, that
supersedes everything else." Thus is community expressed.

Though far from idyllic, Pueblos are places of meaning and belonging that
attach their members to what they can proclaim as my people, my religion, my
history, my Indian self, my place of memory. "What they do not find elsewhere
is the emotional satisfaction of belonging intensely, to which they have been
conditioned and reconditioned" (Eggan 1976:150). What they also do not find
elsewhere is the place that is bounded by their perfectly socialized commitment
to secrecy. Not all Pueblo Indians speak their vernacular, practice their traditional religion, and subscribe to the tribal values that distinguish them from
non-Indians. But all collaborate to provide a secure harbor for Pueblo religion.
This collaboration links them to each other, differentiates them from all non-
Pueblo people, and sustains Pueblo community.

One afternoon I walk through rugged reservation countryside with a Pueblo
father and his adolescent son. The father labors to recover ancestral tribal land
lost by conquest and chicanery. He speaks eloquently of tribal history; he is
knowledgeable about the legal complexities of land issues, aware that his quest,
often thankless, is absolutely necessary. As we walk through landscape marked
by extinct volcanic peaks in the background, his son tries turn-around jumps
on suitable rocky inclines. He is a skateboard enthusiast, and our walk is
occasion for practicing moves that later he will try out on paved streets atop his
skateboard.

A Pueblo student told Anne Smith, "You can't get away from it. You were
brought up in a village … it's handed down, the customs, and you can't get
away from it" (1966:83). A Pueblo man told me, "You know, to be Indian is so

---

[9]No ideal is ever perfectly realized. There are Pueblo people who would join McKnight, an
African American, in saying, "Many of us have assiduously searched for the essence of blackness
and again and again returned to the inner self empty-handed. What does one have to be or do or
believe to be truly, wholly, monolithically black?" (McKnight 1993:107).

good, but it's really hard to be Indian because of all the things you have to put up with." The skateboarding boy has this to learn about himself: if what he finds good about being Indian will be too good to forsake, or if what he finds hard about being Indian will bring him more surely to the world of his skateboard.

A Pueblo mother, employed off her reservation, describes her customary behavior as she drives up to her tribal community:

> Once I get off that freeway, I feel very comfortable, like I'm being embraced by the environment I've just come into. It's, like, my shoes come off, the radar gets unplugged, and the windows rolled down. I can breathe. My son feels that same way. We both go through the same ritual. We both automatically even undo our seat belts, which can be a controversial issue, but that's the way we feel. It's just something about, "Oh, my God!" when I cross the bridge and start seeing people, it's, like, "I'm home."

The tribal community is home to its members, however flawed, however wanting and needy. Ideals, community, home, comfort—these are only half the story.

4

"Caught Up in This Whiteman's Society": Living in Two Worlds

It is possible to live 100% Indian, but it is just the modern things that throw you off.

—*Pueblo student*

People are interested in Indians. They want to know how we've survived so long. We survived the Spanish, Mexicans, and Americans. The Dalai Lama wanted to learn from us because of the Chinese in Tibet.

—*Pueblo educator*

In conventional Pueblo wisdom, urban Indians can choose "to deal with only one life," but as a resident of a tribal community "you have no choice but to live in both worlds." The concept of "both worlds," one Indian, another non-Indian, does not mean that Pueblos think there are only two worlds, each one homogeneous. They well know that the form and expression of their own traditional cultures vary, and also that the non-Indian world just in New Mexico embraces a variety of Indian, Anglo, and Hispanic people. Their reference to "both worlds"[1] masks their actual understanding of cultural heterogeneity.

IN THE MIDST OF SOCIAL CHANGE

I begin a consideration of living in two worlds by briefly overviewing the circumstances of social change that impact Pueblo culture and thus frame Pueblo lives. Historically, the Pueblos could not escape the consequences of immensely intrusive military, religious, and economic invaders. The invaders'

---

[1]Henze and Vanett (1993) question the utility of the two-world metaphor and its assumptions, as do some prominent members of the Pueblo community.

presumptions of cultural superiority were supported by the reality of military superiority. The lines of change introduced by external religious, political, and economic factors increasingly overlaid Pueblo institutions; in time, under contemporary conditions of mass society, all of the non-Indian world came to impinge on Pueblo culture.

The penetration of Pueblo culture has been accomplished by government agents, the purveyors and enforcers of federal policies; by non-Catholic missionaries, so that now Protestantism competes with established Catholic and traditional religious forms; by traders, salesmen, and shopkeepers who bring a splendor of goods to the attention of people who once lived almost self-sufficiently off the land; by tourists, writers, academics, and film makers who want to buy or portray or uncover a people becoming spectacle; by the market economy, and the resulting need for money to satisfy a growing, occasionally resisted, materialism; by the mass media, ever more skilled in presenting abundant alternatives to Pueblo mores and goods; and, not least, by schooling, with its carrots of language, interpersonal skills, and diplomas as the lures to opportunity in the outside world. All this and more has encouraged social change. From causes have come consequences, and consequences have themselves become causes, until distinguishing between the two is hopeless, perhaps unnecessary, in that little is gained beyond knowing that the results are profound, and that the causes and consequences of unrelenting social change are everywhere.

The jumble of interacting cause and consequence establishes social change as an abiding attribute of Pueblo life, so that the nature and meaning of Pueblo tradition is dynamic and complex. Thus to identify what prevails at any given time is to risk misrepresentation, although some changes appear to endure in Pueblo communities.

For example, Pueblo families have been shaped and reshaped by the circumstances of making a living off the reservation. They have also been influenced by the circumstances of divorce, single-parent households, nontraditional households of adult married children preferring to live apart from their parents, and children born of mixed-tribe and mixed-ethnic parents. All of this unsettles Pueblo families, so that there is less time available for them to teach and learn, to discipline and be disciplined; less intimate contact to forge the bonds between young and old; and less occasion for the modeling of desired behavior.

Lamenting these facts, a man from a conservative Pueblo says: "Certain parents, you might say, have loosened some of the proper behavior. One thing happens, and nobody says anything. And the next thing happens, and no one says anything. If it doesn't get corrected, slowly and slowly it gets loosened, and there goes your [traditional] behavior. There goes your respect. It's like people waiting for each other to say something."

To say something, for example, about what, in traditional culture, is expected of parents and children, so that elders are taken care of. In the past, relatives—and not necessarily close ones—were looked after: "You went to see if your mother's cousin had food, wood, water. Nobody teaches caring to kids anymore. It's always *me*, always *us*." To say something so that ceremonies are not lost. A student regrets those ceremonies she knows about that once existed and will probably never come back. "They don't do them anymore because it takes too long and it's a community thing. People are usually at work, or students at school. It takes too much time." And to say something so that young people learn of proper behavior rather than the boldness and rebelliousness by which some defy authority. One adult remarks that "it's not the traditional family unit that it was before," and another that "parents are caught in a bind" between needing to work and needing to spend time with their children.

Striking at the heart of cultural maintenance is the claim of youth that what their parents and elders say or do is "old-fashioned." These words of simple but decisive dismissal reflect a presumed right to judge what is and is not in fashion. "Oh, that was way back," children may say. An adult of old fashion resisting dismissal rejoins, "They don't realize that that's part of the traditional way of life for us. If they'd listen to their elders or anybody from the community, if they would only listen, they could learn a lot." Other adults speak of the restlessness of children during the instructional aspects of ceremonial occasions, and also of the inability of some children to approach adults in the right way: they ask too many questions and don't observe enough.

"If they would only listen." These earnest words of an elder reflect loyalist thinking of people of all ages. They capture the mournful message of a community in flux, though the memory and reality of valued tradition is still robust enough to provide counterpoint to behavior that departs from tradition. In this message is the plea "Don't leave us," a plea that includes, for example, their urban kin: "Since we moved to Albuquerque [New Mexico's largest city, with more than 500,000 people], we see everything different than we do back on the reservation." The message implicitly includes those who don't intend to leave and do not leave the community's physical premises, but whose behavior ignores or challenges tradition and thus signifies their cultural withdrawal. In this regard, potentially, is resistance to some aspects of culture that draws on the changing role of women. As a Pueblo mother commented, "I think the young women of today are trying to obtain opportunities that their mothers never had, and the parents are trying to help them achieve something better." Such sentiments encourage educated, talented women to seek work and accept places in tribal government once occupied only by men. To date, three Pueblo tribes have had a woman governor; this is possible in tribes that elect their governor and highly unlikely in the majority that appoint them.

Still, women can and do occupy many other positions, as I learned when I attended a tribal event for which a program had been prepared that listed all tribal council members and tribal officials. Of 6 council members, one was a woman. Of 26 officials, 9 were women. Four of the 26 were war captains, a position that is too strongly male in conception for a female to be considered eligible. The presence of so many women in positions once filled only by men is a substantial educative fact. It says to everyone, "Look what is possible. Consider what you can aspire to. A new door to opportunity already is open."

Individuals and families seek jobs outside their Pueblos; similarly, the Pueblos themselves seek economic development in order to reduce their reliance on the federal government. The activities of economic development join those associated with securing and recovering land and water rights; the result is an expansion of the secular side of Pueblo communities. Such expansion does not require shrinking the Pueblo's sacred side. It does, however, have an impact: "I think the governors, the secular part, feel more [outside] pressure—the housing, the unemployment, all of those things. They feel more pressure than the traditional ones [the sacred part] that just carry on, carry on. It's like there's a barrier. You handle your part, we'll handle ours."

Personal and communal necessity forces almost everyone into the secular domain, the outside world's market of goods, jobs, and services. Everyone can say, "I need money." Not everyone will say, "I need prayer," or its ceremonial correlates. Everyone can say, "I need the language and learning of school." Not everyone will say, "I need the language and learning of *kiva*." The demand for money and English language proficiency is pressing; the need for prayer and traditional knowledge is more complex and harder to perpetuate.

Between and within school and *kiva*, and outside world and Pueblo world, there are perceptions of mutual usefulness and competing tensions. While taking heart from their culture's half-millennium of survival, Pueblo people live in the shadow of loss. "You hear people talking with neighbors come around. They almost kind of reminisce. They just think back, pause for a moment, and think back, remembering how it was. They start going into all those things about how it was a long time ago. You can see smiles on their faces." Surely, people everywhere recollect past times and smile at what memory has stored up about those times. And, no less surely, what has been lost from past times can be reason for concern about the survival of what remains.

SURVIVAL

If we do not pay attention to the young people, we are going to lose our culture, and they will lose their lives, getting into trouble and drugs. Intruders are always pulling them away. I spend time with young people, dancing and teaching them our songs, because they are forgetting our traditional ways.

—*Governor Jess Mermejo, Jr., Picuris Pueblo*

At an American Indian Week workshop, a Pueblo man spoke of "struggling to survive in a foreign culture," his way of referring to the dominant American mainstream. As I stood watching the Buffalo Dance at Santo Domingo, accompanied by a man from Cochiti whom I had previously been interviewing, I heard him say that when he left his Pueblo's boundary, he entered "another world." Pueblo designation of the non-Indian world as "another world" or a "foreign culture" denotes a place that is more than just physically elsewhere. It is culturally outside their home communities. The outside world is troublesome, possibly hazardous, even when one can say, as one man did, "I have never had a hard time with either world." As a tribal leader of long standing, he knows well that social change and cultural survival challenge his people.

Indian High School board members insisted that I grasp their concern for cultural survival.[2] Accustomed to anthropologists' alerts, for example, to the impact of aggressive agricultural policy on Amazonian tribal people, or to environmentalists' claims about this or that species, I was attuned to remote survival issues. At the school board conference table, I met survival up-close. I could not put away the newspaper, close a book, or turn off the radio and thereby remove the issue from my awareness. At Indian High School, survival would be part of the fabric of my life.

Pueblo youth and adults live with this reality in the way people everywhere live with whatever imminent calamity stalks their habitat—earthquakes, hurricanes, floods, fires, or tornadoes. Physical disasters may be preceded by long, quiet stretches. When they strike, they remind us that we live vulnerably in the wake of what, possibly, we can manage and moderate but never fully control. Cultural disasters may be more insidious, lacking sharply reminding eruptions that call attention to what is always potential. Events contributing to cultural disasters are more like the eroding forces of wind and water that slowly, steadily, endlessly alter the landscape.

Catastrophic events surely can affect cultural loss and survival. At present, such events are not evident in Pueblo life. Tribal loss occurs more certainly from the conduct of a member who, when he becomes an engineer, moves to Texas and rarely returns home, thereby effectively denying his and his family's

---

[2]Notwithstanding Pueblo concerns for survival, anthropologist Alfonso Ortiz (San Juan) analyzes why Pueblo tribes have survived so long and why they continue to survive (1994: 296-306). Theirs has been a unique blend of geographic stability, judicious borrowing and "reseeding," and inventive revitalization.

contributions to their Pueblo. The assurance of survival derives more certainly from the conduct of tribal members who can say, as one student did, "The language that I speak more often is my Indian language. We speak it around little children so that they will grow up to learn a lot about our Indian ways."

I take seriously the school board's caution about survival, reminding myself as I write that beneath the ordinariness of everyday school and community life, of people and institutions naturally conspiring by their routine doings to project images of orderliness, rests a threat of catastrophe. It is rooted in an enduring condition: Pueblo Indians live within a huge society that, on the one hand, is ambivalent about cultural heterogeneity, and, on the other, homogenizes by its great force.

I did not seek to plant an awareness of survival in the consciousness of those I interviewed; I did not need to. Awareness surfaced readily as we spoke about history, language, education, tradition, and grandparents. In short, an abundance of stimuli exist to provoke considerations of survival in people who, unprovoked, manage to live—as do Californians when they suppress and rationalize recollections of the last earthquake—with attention to the reassuring ordinariness of cars and clothing, children and jobs, sports and music. Nevertheless, to ignore or minimize the threats to Pueblo survival would be to observe a movie about war and attend only to its lush landscapes and scenes of romance.

One day, several Indian High School students attended a conference of Indian leaders devoted to land issues. School leaders saw the conference as an opportunity for deepening the understanding of a select group of students who as adults surely would have to deal with comparable issues.

Afterward, a student who attended the conference told me about her day at the meeting: everyone talked about survival, she said, over and over again about survival. Survival here is not a metaphor; it is an abiding situation and condition, like rain, drought, and dancing. She spoke about survival matter-of-factly, although without a hint of cynicism, boredom, or alarm, its gloom so ever present that, for the most part, it operates like background music that is there to hear but ordinarily can be ignored.

Living in its gloom, students know that survival and loss are linked; the gloom has become normal. In retrospect, I believe that it is this fact that moved me to the questions I raise later. They ask, in effect, what can be done? As moths are drawn to flame, so educators are drawn to prospects for change.

In 1907, a writer forecast the future of the Pueblo people: they will disappear because their "whole life becomes transformed, if not degenerated, whenever it touches the life of the white man" (Fynn 1907: 260; see also White 1935 and 1962 and Bruner 1986). Decades later, Dozier considered the life of his people and concluded that "underneath an external surface of modernism" he could see "traditional Pueblo social and cultural patterns" persisting (1964:92). Still later, Simon Ortiz, while facing Fynn's prognosticated darkness, stood firmly by the promise of enduring:

> Survival, I know how this way.
> This way I know....
> We told ourselves over and over
> again, "We shall survive this way." [Ortiz 1975:159]

"This way," of course, is neither Ortiz's nor anyone else's formulated mixture of what is modern and traditional. It is the way of Pueblo tradition, stated but not specified, a way that loves, as he writes, stories, children, mountains, and rain, the uncontested elements of Pueblo life around which one can rally and be cheered. If poetry and stories do rally and cheer, they do not suffice to meet the level of concern expressed by the man who, at his Pueblo, saw the number of tribal leaders declining and tradition inadequately encouraged. His response: "It scares me. We're all losing everything, seems like."

This response points to the scourge of assimilation, the long-time official federal government policy for the schooling of Indian children (see Ortiz 1987; Spicer 1962; and Moyers 1941). And assimilation, however gently stated and seemingly enlightened its rationale, leads to cultural disappearance. To traditionalists, it is plague, cataclysm, a magician's master trick: now you see 'em, now you don't. It is chronic, ultimately fatal, as "a culture creeps nearer to absorption, to a transformation that also means demise" (Carter 1993:76)—though not the merciful demise, say, of a large bomb's direct hit, but rather that of a wasting illness.

For Pueblo Indians, survival is a haunting issue. To a mother, it is couched in physical terms, of a generation of her tribe's children born with fetal alcohol syndrome (see Dorris 1989) that she knows has devastated native groups elsewhere in the country. Her concern builds on the too-real fear of rampant alcoholism. To a tribal leader, it is couched in secular terms, revealing his uncertainty about his tribe's children accepting the responsibilities of tribal maintenance: "I started letting the kids know, 'You are my future, you are my tomorrow. Learn all you can at Indian High School. Get your diploma. Be a lawyer, be a doctor, be an engineer, and then I will be safe. I want to make sure I am in good hands when you are the future.' I am not too secure [he says sadly]. I see some of our youth still into a lot of things."

Teachers and students join the mother and the tribal leader in wishing that Indian High School students cared more and wished to learn more about their Pueblo cultures, and, though somewhat forgiven as adolescents, that they cared less about dressing well, contemporary music, and driving new cars or trucks.

They might also wish that Indian High School students would get matters somewhat clearer than the student who spoke with his heart in the right place and a garbled sense of time: "Our culture is still here, but in another hundred years I think it would be gone. That's why us young Indians especially have a lot of responsibilities in our villages, so our Indian ways will live on forever."

The public surfaces of Pueblo life are not filled with references to survival. Neither at school nor in the communities is it a topic invariably encountered in the course of an ordinary day. However grim its implications, it is less tangible, say, than homework and tests, or dates, food, and dancing; by any measure, it is decidedly more imponderable. Beneath the surface, however, lies an awareness of survival. When stimulated by a class assignment, students can write about their Indian ways living on forever, and the hovering threat of demise.

Young and old responded in almost formulaic language about the issues of survival, as if from a common script. They spoke of the language–religion connection: if our language is lost, so will be our religion, and then our culture;[3] and of the education–land connection: if we don't educate our own lawyers, we won't successfully defend our land interests, and without our land, our community is lost. The prevalence of such connections and the ease with which discussion of survival was elicited persuaded me that it was indeed a spectre among Pueblo people, too awful to live with as palpable daily fare, but nonetheless a defining fact of life.

The expressions of some students sounded like the pieties of those who had long heard the refrain "don't forget who you are or where you come from," and who knew the propriety of despairing about their future. Most often, however, the despair rang true, and I would try to imagine how it must feel to love a culture and community about which one could say both "If the language goes, then a large part of the culture goes, too," and "At my Pueblo, there are not any people under the age of twenty that I really know who speak the language fluently." Or, as another student says, "Language is the key. It just permeates every part of you. Oh, yes, it's scary. In my own family, I have cousins that don't understand the language. They come home for the sacred doings. They are just there physically. Spiritually and emotionally they cannot understand."

In the past, when virtually all people spoke their tribal language, its necessity was confirmed beyond doubt; no basis existed for thinking otherwise. Circumstances of invasion, conquest, and culture contact have placed Pueblo people

---

[3]The vernacular maintenance–cultural survival connection is commonplace in the literature. See Suina and Smolkin (1994), *Indian Nations at Risk* (1991), and Emerson (1995).

in a dual-language setting, establishing occasion in the past to speak Spanish, and most recently to speak English. What was a matter of personal circumstance in the case of Spanish is a matter of near inevitability in the case of English: today, everyone must speak and be literate in English. And inevitability joins with the disposition of Pueblo Indians to mix within the 19 tribes and with other, non-Pueblo tribes. Cross-tribal interaction at school, work, and eventually in marriage creates families in which parents are unable to speak the same Indian language. This makes English the common language of the home and often leaves children with little to no fluency in any Indian language. The turn to English has been further advanced by the decision some families make that their children learn English as their first language, believing that economic success requires facility in English, not in their vernacular: "My dad believed in education. And in order for us to be educated to the best, we had to speak English first."

English has become the medium for intertribal discussion, as it has for many families and tribes. The tribes today present an often complex language scene, ranging from those Pueblos where one is scolded for publicly speaking any language but the vernacular to those where English usage rivals or surpasses the vernacular. With few exceptions—some old people and more youngsters who will not learn English until they attend Head Start—everyone knows English; some older people know Spanish from the days when Spanish was the major non-Indian language spoken in New Mexico.

A Pueblo student justified what he called the "Anglo curriculum" of Indian High School: "The reason they teach it is that we have to have it to live with a dominant race. If we don't have it, people will just run right over us. If we don't know what they are talking about, we won't be able to defend ourselves." That he must have such defensive awareness worries Indian High School's Pueblo educators who do not doubt its necessity, but are saddened by feeling obliged to burden their students with it: "I feel like the same thing was done to me. I have no choice. The future of the tribe rests on each individual person." These educators transmit to their students what students hear their grandparents say: "I worry about how it will be the day we close our eyes, if we will always continue on, knowing the things we need to know."

Living in two worlds frames the issue of cultural survival. Learning about holding on and giving up in the process of cultural remaining and becoming are threads in the unfolding tapestry of Pueblo life. The process enjoys neither master designer nor grand design. Tribal communities lay claim to priorities; tribal individuals lay claim to needs. Each entails responsibilities.

The process is marked more by eloquence than by the pull of clear, convincing direction.

CONCEPTIONS OF DUAL-WORLD LIVES

Interest in the learning of more than one culture has attracted a profusion of social science, fiction, and memoir writers,[4] perhaps especially in the United States where the phenomenon of cultural remaining and becoming never ceases to be a vital issue, often harshly vital. Notwithstanding the resulting gush of words, each ethnic subgroup undergoes its dual-world experiences on its own, struggling to endure, define, clarify, rectify, and enjoy what it encounters in this never easy, always challenging process. Somehow, it matters little that many have previously marched down the dual-world road. The march of others before you seldom informs you. Your march is unique, to be worked out, for better or worse, on your terms, such as you can and are allowed to manage them. Being "allowed to" refers to those external social, political, and economic limits often imposed by one's prejudiced predecessors to the march.

I take for granted that Pueblo people have a conception, however contested, of living in two worlds, and that it is a given in their lives. "Living in two worlds," a shorthand expression, contains sufficiently shared meaning not to require clarification for ordinary usage.[5] Indian High School students needed no explanation when asked to write or talk about it. It is mentioned in Pueblo publications. For example, the 1994 official visitors guide called Eight Northern Indian Pueblos contained a picture of two preschool boys sitting on the steps of a house, one with a large baseball mitt in his hand, the other holding a play gun and wearing a Levi's T-shirt. The caption under their picture read, "Our children grow up in two cultures whose values often are in conflict." Newspapers reflect this usage—"Navajo surgeon learns to operate in two

---

[4]See, for example, Lorene Cary's *Black Ice*, Frank Chin's *Donald Duk*, Gish Jen's *Typical American*, David Mura's *Turning Japanese*, Eva Hoffman's *Lost in Translation*, and Richard Rodriguez's *Hunger of Memory*.

[5]Non-Indian writers have spoken of their two-world lives, often with anguish. Among the most notable is W.E.B. DuBois's much quoted *cri du coeur*: "One ever feels his twoness ... two souls, two thoughts, two unreconciled strivings; two warring ideals in one dark body" (1969:45). Eva Hoffman quotes Mary Antin, "It is painful to be consciously of two worlds" (in Hoffman 1989:163). An important recent contribution to the discussion of "double consciousness" is Early's *Lure and Loathing: Essays on Race, Identity, and the Ambivalence of Assimilation* (1993). See also Kugelmass's *Between Two Worlds: Ethnographic Essays on American Jewry* (1988).

cultures" (Foehr 1994:3); "Vigil Gray [Jicarilla Apache] has stepped into his own limelight. It is one distinguished by a relentless passion to straddle the two tenacious and opposing worlds he inhabits" (Bentley 1995:60); as do journals—"Nowhere is [change] more evident than in the students' voices as they learn to … exist in two cultures …" (Kaufman 1994:4).

Beyond the everyday use of the two-world notion is a complexity belied by the ease with which Pueblo young and old use the term. I struggle for some level of clarity, persuaded of the necessity to do so because I assume a close relationship between the fact of this dualism and understanding the response of Pueblo youth to schooling. I also assume that though this dualism is a commonplace fact in the lives of Indian High School's Pueblo students, its application as a positively or negatively determining factor in the life of a particular person is beyond my data.

As is true, unsurprisingly, of the complex aspects of our lives, my Pueblo interviewees got relatively better in their articulations of this phenomenon the longer we spoke, but it remained, ultimately, in a hard-to-penetrate black box. It lacked the type of formal clarification I heard fundamentalist Christian students receive about their life in two worlds, one sacred and wonderful, the other secular, treacherous, and requiring constant vigilance for the sacred to prevail. Christian students were constantly indoctrinated in school and church about why they were Christians, and just exactly how they were to think and behave as Christians, in contrast with those of us who are not. The Christian rationale was explicit, accessible to the slightest query, and, generally, unambiguously forthright. Pueblo duality does not enjoy such straightforward elaboration.

To begin my own clarification of the dual-world concept, I locate the Indian and non-Indian worlds within the matrix presented in Fig. 4.1. Having done so, I must at once explain that there are multiple orientations within each cell; moreover, the plus and minus signs and the signs themselves are ambiguous.

Nonetheless, at the simplest level, the double-plus Cell 1 contains those people who by choice and accomplishment live in and are more or less successful in both worlds. The fact of choice is meant to indicate that individuals may have a personal preference about where they desire to locate their life. The fact of accomplishment is meant to indicate that judgments are made about how well one lives or performs in one world or the other or both. This "success" is remarked on most positively by fellow Pueblos; it is a compliment to be identified as successful in both worlds. Conversely, the double-minus Cell 4 contains people who have failed in both worlds, their failure manifest by unemployment, social rejection, and unhappiness wherever they are. Cells 2 and 3 contain those who are successful basically in either the non-Indian or Indian world, respectively, their lives, by virtue of choice, chance, or skill, more definitely oriented to one or the other world, but not to both. Success and failure are relative terms. They suggest personal dispositions toward or away from one or the other world, and circumstantial fortune or misfortune in the affairs of each world.

Taken more complexly, and thus more realistically, the particulars of a life located within each cell relate, as I see them, to several different matters (the multiple orientations refer to the foregoing). These matters, the basis for deciding how to locate someone within the matrix, include the following:

1. Where geographically a person spends her time, that is, where she lives, works, plays, shops, visits, and so on. Clearly, the dual-world concept includes the physical locations of one's life.
2. What culture a person has learned. This relates to the possible cultural variants—Indian and non-Indian—that one has been subject to as formal and informal learner, derived from home, community, school, work, media, and peer sources.
3. How a person lives. The point above refers to acquired culture content; this one refers to how a person actually lives his life. A person may know how to behave in ways appropriate to some cultural setting but have neither occasion nor intention to use what he has learned.
4. How competently a person performs in each world. The measures of competence can be taken from either world, with different conclusions about competence thereby resulting.
5. How a person feels about each world, if she likes where geographically and culturally she lives, and where her heart and concerns for the future are. Where she lives is separable from the issue of how she feels about where she lives.

To begin to capture the breadth of dual-world possibilities for a particular person, I would need to construct a matrix like Fig. 4.1 based on the facts underlying each

Indian World

		+	−
Non-Indian World	+	(1) +/+	(2) +/−
	−	(3) −/+	(4) −/−

FIG. 4.1. Central tendencies of Pueblo Indian dual-world orientations.

of these five matters. In this way I could show, for example, (1) that a certain Pueblo man spends most of his time in his Pueblo community, an Indian plus; (2) that since he grew up in the city, he learned most about non-Indian culture, a non-Indian plus; (3) that as a young man, he became reconnected with his father's tribe and now endeavors to live in an Indian way, an Indian plus; (4) that his cultural competence lies essentially in affairs of the non-Indian world, where his primary socialization occurred, a non-Indian plus; but, finally, (5) that he has become so lopsidedly attached to his newfound Pueblo life that he is devoted to his tribal community, an Indian plus. The picture of this hypothetical man that emerges from considering the five matters is useful but limited. Simple plus and minus indicators of central tendency do injustice to the degrees of importance that can be given to a fact.

A person whose general behavior seemingly locates her in a particular cell can sometimes behave, because of situational circumstances, in a way unfitting for that cell. Moreover, because of long-term prevailing circumstances, a person's behavior eventually may change sufficiently to locate her in a cell other than where she once had been. In short, one's dual-world life is dynamic, even though it is located in one of the four cells at any given time. It embraces where one lives, the culture one has learned, the culture one lives, and with what degree of competence and caring.[6] Nonetheless, the Pueblo ideal focuses essentially, but not exclusively, on the double pluses of cell 1, in recognition of the general inevitability of a dual-world life and the wish that in each world the person's usual behavior will bring success.

Indian High School's commitment, shared by its 19 Pueblo host communities, is that its students learn to "walk" competently in each world.[7] This view enjoys consensus support and acceptance in these broadly defined terms—obtaining the best possible education and as good a job as one can achieve, while sincerely participating to the fullest in one's tribal activities, and accepting the primacy of tribal over personal well-being. It incorporates the Pueblo indicators of good citizenship. It is a much-publicized ideal in Pueblo socializing circles. A person praised as living well in both worlds approximates this behavior.

---

[6]Another way to configure the pluses and minuses is Oetting and Beauvais's orthogonal identification model, which by allowing a person to be located positively or negatively on any dimension of behavior or affect in one or both worlds precludes the either–or necessity of other models (1990–1991). See also LaFromboise, Coleman, and Gerton (1993) for a most useful discussion of different models that relate to dual identity.

[7]LaFromboise, Coleman, and Gerton discuss the notion of competence at length (1993: 403–9). Their "dimensions" include "(a) knowledge of cultural beliefs and values; (b) positive attitudes toward both majority and minority groups; (c) bicultural efficacy; (d) communication ability; (e) role repertoire; and (f) a sense of being grounded" (1993:403).

School and Pueblo leaders want their youth to be cell-1 citizens, but with the Pueblo plus preeminent. As taken-for-granted exceptions, everyone understands that some sacred and secular tribal positions necessitate spending most of one's time on the reservation, and that some sacred tribal positions may be filled by persons (cell 3, –/+) who have little skill in the outside world, but possess all the requisite skills for their Indian world.[8] Everyone also understands that the meaning and expression of dual-world (cell-1) competence and participation draw upon different conceptions of religious orthodoxy and therefore differ from tribe to tribe, and from person to person. Given effective learning in each world, one could properly be labelled *bicultural,*[9] though I seldom heard this term used. School and Pueblo value such accomplishment, as long as one's heart remains Indian and assimilation in the non-Indian world is discouraged.[10] In short, bicultural competence is fine, bicultural loyalty is not.

Fully distant from the double-plus promise of cell one is the double-minus disappointment of cell 4, for which designation I obtained a set of linking verbs, but none of them from my interviewees. By the chance of who I met, I heard no one speak about himself or others in this despairing cell in the language that I had often read. Scheper-Hughes referred to certain Pueblo adults who "un-

---

[8]Pueblo people fondly identify tribal members who had little to no success of any consequence at school, currently occupy relatively menial positions outside their reservations, but are leaders of note in their own communities: "He was never academically inclined; he only did what he had to do when it comes to education. When it comes to the traditional, that's where his mind is."

[9]Related terms are *biculturation*—"the socialization of individuals into two or more cultures in a situation of stabilized pluralism" (Polgar 1960:233), and *biculturism*—the behavior of one who "cross[es] cultural boundaries ... operating first within one ethnic group and then within another or on the edges between both ... [In] such settings, people master knowledge of both" (Clifton 1989:29).

[10]Such a position is comparable to what Ramirez calls a "functional multicultural/Latino orientation," whereby a person "functions competently in both Latino and mainstream cultures [and] feels more comfortable and self-assured in Latino culture" (in Rotheram-Borus 1993:84), and to what LaFromboise, Coleman, and Gerton call their alternation model of biculturalism (1993: 399–400. The cell-1 form appears to be the preference of ethnic subgroups that choose to sustain their ethnic distinctiveness. Its actual manifestation will be influenced by the extent of cultural distinctiveness of a subgroup, with extent occupying a continuum that would place, say, Americans of French or English descent at the minimum pole and Americans of Indian, orthodox Jewish, or Amish descent at the maximum pole. Location anywhere on the continuum depends on the availability of sanctioned alternatives within the subgroup that contrast with cultural expressions in the dominant society, regarding, for example, "living habits, the values they place on aspects of living, and the goals they set for themselves" (McNickle, quoted in Walker 1972:123). Ramirez' full conception has four forms, ranging from "monocultural" to "synthesized multicultural" (in Rotheram-Borus 1993).

successfully straddl[e][11] the two worlds" (1987:65). Henze and Vanett graphically depict the straddling metaphor in their conclusion about the Native American Yup'iks of Alaska: "picture an individual struggling to walk with one foot on one side of a river bank and the other foot on the other side, with a raging torrent in the middle. It would be an impossible task" (1993:130).

Whether one is "stranded" (Lafromboise and Bigfoot 1988:146), "suspended" (Clifton 1989:28), or "split down the middle, with one foot in Indian culture and one in the modern world" (Smith 1966:22), the outcome is an unfortunate person. He is most often labeled "marginal," and characterized as "one who lives in two worlds, in both of which he is more or less a stranger" (Robert E. Park, quoted in Levine 1985:75), or one who is "unable to identify with either the new culture or the old, and mill[s] about in a no-man's land—socially, emotionally, intellectually" (Spindler and Spindler 1971:10). In these conceptions, the marginal person is indeed unfortunate, a stranger without a functional cultural identity, a candidate for one form of self-destruction or another.

Cells 2 (+/–) and 3 (–/+) of Fig. 4.1 are logical places in any matrix of this type. The former represents the stronger presence of the non-Indian world, the latter of the Indian world. I heard about cell-2's assimilated men and women, usually someone's relatives who had left the reservation, never returned, never brought their children back, never participated in any form. They had, it seemed, departed physically and culturally, perhaps looking like an Indian but not living like one. The Spindlers wrote about such persons among the Menomini of Wisconsin. They had "move[d] to an identification with the dominant system irrespective of its divergence [from the traditional cultural system]" (1971:10).

I also heard about cell-3 persons (–/+).[12] They were very old, spoke no or little English, and had long confined their lives to their Pueblos, sustained in their homes, as all Pueblo people are, by the material goods of the outside world (including a television set that seems always to be on), but otherwise contained within the boundaries of their tribal culture. A Pueblo educator identified another type of cell-3 person as someone who chose "not to live and succeed in the city or in Anglo society, and is content to work within the tribe, work[ing] for the community and feel[ing] more comfortable doing that." Such people can be found among students. As one said of himself: "I do not feel any push or pull between the two worlds because I only focus on one world, which is my Indian religion .... I will only belong to one world until the day I die." Some religious leaders may be cell-3 persons.

---

[11]I see "straddle" used in literature that refers to the lives of immigrants and other minorities. For example, see Lopate's review of Lorene Cary's book *Black Ice* (1991:7) and Ugna-Oju (1993:400).

[12]See Bruner (1956) for another version of a cell-3 (–/+) type person.

I learned about the Pueblo dual-world experience in many ways, not least by attending to the verbs they used to clarify how they thought the two worlds were joined. I uncovered no pervasive wisdom about the "right" linking verb, though I heard often about the sweetly hypnotic "select the best of both worlds," a resolution that instantly sounds sensible, in the self-evident category of thinking, but does not hold up to careful scrutiny (see Henze and Vanett 1993). "I took the good and left the bad," says Lakota medicine man Charles Fast Horse in a newspaper interview (Jones 1991:16), which suggests a conscious act of choosing from a dual-world behavioral menu that seems farfetched, though not just for Mr. Fast Horse.[13] Perhaps unfortunately, much of who we are we learned to be long before we were aware of choices, and by the time we are aware, we face stiffly narrowed possibilities for choosing. Furthermore, what is "best" in each of the two worlds is a controversial matter, as is what one does with the bests that one has chosen, to continue with this mechanical representation of how a self gets constructed. I labor the point because it so often is advanced as the answer to the dual-world challenge, an answer that slights the collectivist orientation of Pueblo communities.

The linking verb of choice seems to be *balance.* A Pueblo woman speaks of her dual-world awareness: "I know there is a distinction that I make myself of who I am, depending on where I am and what I am doing," and then she addresses the link: "I really have tried to balance it all," concentrating on what she has to do either at home or at work. Or, as a Pueblo man perceives: "If you choose one or the other [world], then you can't really quite balance them. It takes elements from both to survive in the Pueblo community or in the mainstream." Perhaps "balance" occurs to him and others because of the Pueblo attraction to balance and harmony as traditional ideals that they now apply to the expanded cultural realities of their lives.

A strong but less frequently heard alternative to that of balancing two worlds holds that, "If you are well-grounded in your roots as an Indian, you don't live in two worlds, you live in one. Wherever I am, I take with me the values that I learned from [my] community." Its advocates argue that, of course, they "make adjustments" if they go, say, to the city, even to another Pueblo, "but my basic point is that who I am didn't change. My basic values don't change."

I cannot sort out whether the differences in conception between living in two worlds or one, as just expressed, are merely semantic. "Adjustment" does seem to capture a sense of those behavioral modifications and accommodations that

---

[13]Charles Fast Horse is not alone: "Lucy Tapahonso, a poet who writes about her Navajo culture…simply makes the best of it, taking from each place what each has to offer" (Cone 1994:25). And in another example drawn from the Navajo world: *"Beyond the Four Corners of the World* ends with the Bedonies still searching for balance. Measured against their lives, the glib claim that people caught between two cultures can somehow choose the best from each seems a bitter taunt" (deBuys 1995:39).

we all make as we move from one behavioral domain to another (from home to work to church to bowling, etc.), and present ourselves in terms appropriate for each domain. The one-world-adjustment believers may be emphasizing an aspect of two-world living that should be added to the latter's ideal: that Pueblo values should be so well-taught that they operate as constants in all of one's behavior, wherever one happens to be. In this notion, non-Indian acculturation extends to externals—to the adoption of behavior required to be socially acceptable or to do a job well in the outside world, whereas Indian socialization embraces external and internal matters, both behavior and beliefs and values. A Pueblo student caught this distinction, clarifying that though she probably would have to work, maybe even live, outside her Pueblo after graduation, she meant to live "all in one," an undivided self. "How do you do that?" I ask her. "You just have to have it in your spirit," she replies.

Finally, a student depicts an ideal dual-world person with a maturity and insight cheering to those who otherwise might despair of the intentions and understandings of youth:

> I cannot survive without my education and I cannot live without my Indian values. The reason why I cannot live without my education is because of the rapidly changing world. I cannot live without my Indian values, as well, because they provide the spiritual support I need to live a harmonious life. Though the differences set them apart in different worlds, they are balanced in myself and I try to equally participate in both worlds. The balance of cultures and the participation in both worlds make me the person who I am, an Indian learning of the new technologies of the world and keeping in tune with the old traditions of my people.

A four-cell matrix[14] is a simple representation of an inordinately complex matter. It cannot capture the enormous variability in the ways young and old,

---

[14]Other conceptions of what this matrix is basically about—socialization, acculturation, and assimilation—are available in Spindler and Spindler (1971:10); Henze and Vanett (1993:124); Bruner (1953:26–9); Luftig (1983:256), LaFromboise, Coleman, and Gerton (1993: 396–401); and Oetting and Beauvais (1990–1991: 659–62). Moreover, Henze and Vanett (1993) clarify how important it is to get one's metaphor straight, concluding that the simplistic "walk in two worlds" they saw used by the Yup'ik is problematic: "the language used to express these goals [for schooling], although seemingly benign, is a powerful force shaping people's expectations of students and their view of the worlds around them. When a metaphor such as walking in two worlds reduces and distorts the options of young people, their future is damaged" (1993:131). A Pueblo leader believes similarly that perpetuating the two-world metaphor may create uncertainty: "If you start teaching people to live in two worlds, you start throwing those kinds of concepts around. First of all, you are confusing the already confused kid who has doubts, and maybe throwing some doubt into those kids who thought they had it down: 'Hey, I thought I knew who I was and suddenly I find I'm supposed to live in two worlds.'"

male and female, educated and uneducated, tradition-oriented and non-tradition-oriented persons compose their lives. The matrix draws on the Pueblo characterization of themselves as people who live in two worlds. They believe that the issue is not if they will do so, but how. "How" incorporates the five matters I noted earlier.

DUAL-WORLD ATTRIBUTIONS

"I have the power to be Indian or non-Indian," exclaimed a Pueblo student. "I would be Indian at home and non-Indian away from home." No hint of struggling tinges this testimonial to adolescent will, no sound of tackling decisions that challenge one to choose between competing claims for time, for where to go, for whom to serve and be. Would that he had the power.... Closer to home is a more elaborated reality.

Are there differences between the two worlds? Must I behave differently in each? Are the differences clear-cut? A Pueblo student clarifies her sense of two worlds: "OK, I think this would be a good example. You can sleep in all directions pertaining to the white world. In ours, you can't sleep with your head to the east. We bury our people to the east; it's always been like that. Many times I forget and I sleep that way and I get terrible headaches. [This happens] not just because you know about it. It doesn't matter where you are at. It is always there." This student perceives a stubborn condition—no matter where she is, there is a right way to sleep that, if violated, has unpleasant consequences. Yet, she knows well that traditional life at her Pueblo has changed, and is changing. Meanwhile, what currently exists, exists with authority, even as the "eternal" slips away.

Authority for rightness outside the Pueblo lies in a non-Indian out there, with those who are its citizens (and male citizens, at that): "Your everyday things, like what you do and what you say, you have to look at it from two different views. 'How will that person react to what I do now? Does he think I am being stupid, or stuff like that?' You have to think in a way that a non-Indian person would understand." Her cultural starting point in life is as an Indian, as it is for those born and raised in their tribal communities. It could be a shaky starting point if weakened by indeterminacy and conflict in the lives of those who raised her, but it is nonetheless primary.

Her fellow student clarifies this point by way of contrasting her own sense of self:

When you are younger, they teach you more about the Pueblo, your language, your tradition, and what goes on. When you get older, you start learning a new language, and you don't know why you have to learn English. What is so important? When you are smaller, you grow up with your Indian name and everything is Indian. Then you go to school.

For her and others, attending school is likely to be the first thoroughgoing occasion for culture contact beyond the tribe. By the end of her high school years, she can speak unhesitatingly about having "to learn to live like an Anglo, you know, you pay taxes and do things for the government," but her distinctions about the two worlds tellingly locate her soul:

> It is natural to go home and live on the reservation and just be a regular Indian. You don't have to impress people, like you do in the Anglo world. [Where] you are a minority, you have to really make an impression to people that you are not all that bad of a person, like people say you are. It's just wanting to get noticed for what you really are.... I want to go out and get an education and prove to people that Indians are smart, and they actually have the ability to do something with their lives.

She is "natural" and "regular" in one setting; she must "prove" and "impress" in the other. With her life so framed, she calmly announces her intention to get educated and set the record straight. About her earlier necessity to learn English she asked, "What is so important?" In early childhood, English related to nothing she knew or understood. Today, she can glibly, affirmatively, answer this question. Among taxes and other things, the outside world is a place for proving oneself and straightening records.

Not all students and adults frame their two worlds in the same terms. They might converge, however, around several distinctions, for example, of their Indian world as sacred and, seemingly, unchanging in its values, and of the non-Indian world as secular and "like a big gust of wind. One day you may pick a bunch of leaves and come back the next day and the pile is different. The non-Indian world is always changing." Each world, moreover, has its particular utility: "We, the people of my Pueblo, do dances and secret ceremonies to thank Father-Sun and Mother-Earth for the life of the Indian way. When a dance is done, it is for thanks. In return you will get a longer life." Rewards from "the Indian way" of "a longer life" are set beside the outside world's education, work, and material gain.

Students describe the two worlds in contrasting terms, as I learned when I asked them to think of all the words that came to mind when they imagined "the Pueblo world" and the "outside world." The students were sophomores, juniors, and seniors, about 40 in number, almost 10% of the high school's enrollment. I had interviewed each of them before. I prepared them for the task by asking them to word associate with their favorite sport; all Indian High School students have a favorite sport. Once assured that they grasped the procedure, I began with one stimulus or the other—"Pueblo world" or "outside world." Students were about equally prolific in generating responses to each stimulus. Some could not or would not think much about bringing words to mind; others seemed as if they could go on forever. What resulted, in any event, were spur-of-the-moment responses to my request, "When I say ['outside world' or 'Pueblo world'], you just say what words come to mind." And they did, the results reinforcing the positions they have ready at hand to characterize each world. In Table 4.1, I offer several sets of the positions (each set from the same student) to establish the flavor of the students' responses.

If the sampling in Table 4.1 does not exhaust all the distinctions students made, it basically elaborates their view of one place of family, home, and tradition, and another of jobs, goods, danger, and expectation. This assortment

TABLE 4.1

Student Dual-World Responses

Student	To Outside World	To Pueblo World
1	job, money, rent, danger, killings, racism	safe, parents
2	money, competition, malls, opportunities, schools	elderly, horses, dances, feast days, moccasins, grandpa, *kiva*
3	fast, hard to live, lots of people, have to succeed, business, complete opposite of Pueblo	house, family, mesas, dance, *kiva*, friends, at home
4	jobs, cars, signs, stores, school, college, clothes, shoes, gangs, parties, people	cool, glad, happy, tribal memories, clans, traditional government, arts and crafts, tradition, elderly
5	other people, different places, jobs, big business, interesting, kind of want to get experience	family, friends, dances, feasts, houses, land
6	sports cars, expensive clothes, jobs, reality, struggle, scared, lost	drinking, family, tradition, unemployment, houses, food, dancing

of attributes suggests what is involved when Pueblos construct their dual-world identity, a construction that Table 4.1 exaggerates because these students were not invited to contemplate points of similarity between the two worlds.

Nonetheless, by whatever means I inquired, the students' worlds were poles apart. The balancing, the straddling, or, somehow, the integrating they and others seem to expect of themselves, emerges as an immense and difficult undertaking. One world relates to technology, economics, the future, and, as a student expressed, "turning myself into something I ain't, but something I want to become" among non-Indians who "are mainly concerned with theirselves and nothing or no one around them." How curious, and sad, that he speaks of wanting to become someone he is not for a world that he disparages! The student's "ain't" is a joke; his self-assessment is not. His world relates to "learning to be with nature and learning one's self"; where "you're expected more than you are in the whiteman's world, expected just to participate and be very sacred"; and where "I have more to think about and understand our ways much better so I could pass it on." His idealization ignores the problems that plague all Pueblos, but that is another matter.

From within these distinctions, I see addressed the requirements of survival. One world considers serious economic matters that demand skill if not personal transformation for personal success; the other considers serious matters of self and community for a future that belongs to the past of revered tradition, a past worthy of transmission. Unmentioned are any elements of the outside world that would invite Pueblo concern for their transmission. They remain mere elements, the incidental pieces of someone else's life. This distinction bears an awful irony: Pueblo youth are expected to master elements of the non-Pueblo world of becoming, but these elements are not graced with Pueblo approval. The Pueblo left hand fully acknowledges the necessity of its non-Pueblo right hand, but refuses generally to accept its accomplishments as culturally legitimate.[15]

Pueblo students may take varied paths to arrive at a crossroad of uncertainty about their duality. I cite two lengthy excerpts in order to convey in their own words what is most graphic to them. Both are stated by sophomores, the first by a boy, the second by a girl:

> The Indian world is more complex to understand. Indian people are more tied to
> the environment and spiritual world. In the non-Indian world people are more

---

[15]There is more to this matter. Pueblo people do take pride in their tribal fellows who, because of different, and not necessarily monetary, accomplishments, have achieved success in the outside world. They also take pride in, and see the necessity of, those whose outside-world skills enable them to be defenders and enablers of tribal well-being. Uncertainty about how to hold these accomplishments in relation to one's Indian self and community is what raises the point of cultural legitimacy.

advanced in technology.... I'm more successful in the Indian world because that's the world I grew up in. I would like to be more successful in the non-Indian world, because it pays more money. It is also more challenging to the Indians. I think that most Indians are successful in the Indian world rather than the non-Indian world.... The world that is pushing me is the Indian world, because it wants me to learn more about the non-Indian world. With this I am kind of confused because Indians say that we should keep our traditions.

Non-Indians want us to have an education. They don't realize that we too have an obligation to survive and hunger to be at our best. Living in both worlds is like comparing an eagle and computers. The eagle is Indian, it's free but wise. The computer brainwashes and doesn't care.... I'm about successful in the non-Indian [world] because I was raised this way. My parents didn't want to be humiliated so we [were] raised the white way. Now it's even more ostracizing because we can't communicate to our elders or know stories of the past. I feel as being stuck in the non-Indian world. I can't communicate in the Indian world. This is what I regret as being white, an apple, meaning white inside, Indian outside. This brings a lot of discomfort and anger.

The boy is confused by the apparent contradiction between feeling simultaneously pushed "to learn more about the non-Indian world" and urged to "keep our tradition." What might be clear to those who advocate this behavior is not clear to him. Indeed, even if it becomes perfectly clear, he might not know how to reconcile the competing claims from each world. The girl is angry because her parents chose to emphasize the non-Indian side of their lives. With this emphasis achieved, she feels culturally lost, yearningly aware of her Indian heritage, but not able to inhabit it. Perhaps able to earn "more money" in the non-Indian world, she discounts the value of this "success" because of opportunities denied in her tribal life.

When students were asked to write essays in their English class about their two-world lives, they often were moved to eloquence and strong feeling: "A world of anger, a world of hatred, a world in a state of confusion, the world of the non-Indian hurts all that we respect. The Indian world is a world in which the community is living in harmony." Though such caricatures damage by their respective defaming and flattering simplification, they must be taken as the serious outlook of some Pueblo people, their course of dual-world clarification perhaps unduly complicated by so believing. A more fruitful (granted, more tiring) outlook is expressed by a senior girl: "What is my world like? This question goes through my mind every day of my life." She exaggerates, of course, but her questioning, her knowing, moreover, that she must question, may equip her with the disposition to explore, weigh, try out, and abandon understandings and behaviors that appear as candidates for her consideration. In short, she may be better endowed to ponder the dual-world puzzles she experiences. By her exaggeration, she expresses a profound personal fact.

I close this section with a brief discussion of some further elements of Pueblo duality. In regard to the element of religion, most Pueblo people observe both Catholicism and their traditional religion. Over the centuries that both faiths have coexisted in tribal life, they have become interwoven in practice, with no apparent doctrinal conflict.[16] The Indian students I interviewed clarified that they believed in their Pueblo and Catholic religions, and they saw no conflict between the two. Most did not see Catholicism as a religion of white people. Prayers offered via either religion can be heard. A Pueblo woman clarifies a commonly held position: "I have kind of understood how the Catholic and the Indian religion are parallel. How they are both the same thing, intermingling and overlapping. Older people in the Pueblos make the connections for us. I understand that we are going in the same direction." She sees a smooth, conjoined effort in her two religious identities, one directed by her own people, the other directed by white priests.

On taking office, tribal officials receive blessings from each of their faiths, and weddings integrate procedures drawn from each. Parents identify principles of good conduct that find support in each: "I remember my mom always telling me that you treat other people the way you want them to treat you. This is just exactly what it says in the Bible, and that is exactly what they say in Indian." While some individuals favor one religion over the other, others comfortably model devotion to each, as in the case of a Pueblo office manager and former governor: "First thing every morning when I arrive, I open [the office] up and I say the daily prayer, and then I ask my co-workers if they want me to share with them what the contents was. But I also remind them I did the other part. I prayed with the cornmeal before I left the house to come to work." As regards religion itself, the most complex and sensitive aspect of Pueblo life, there is, apparently, the most successful dual-world integration.

Like religion, language is another central element in Pueblo duality, and also not a matter of complicated or contentious reconciling. "At my [reservation] day school," said a student, "if we would talk our language, they would always tell us, 'English please.'" This request does not carry the sting of an earlier generation's day school efforts to eradicate the vernacular in the name of assimilation. Today, the requirement of English-language competence is virtu-

---

[16]The current rapprochement between Catholicism and Pueblo religion follows centuries of persecution and conversion, on the one hand, and hostility, resentment, and resistance, on the other (see Ortiz 1969; Spicer 1962). The syncretic Catholicism of Pueblo tribes is testimony, among other things, to the unsurprising endurability of the Catholic church and the Pueblos profound commitment to their traditional religion.

ally beyond dispute, as is that of tribal-language competence. Each has its place, and since the places do not overlap, there is no necessary competition between them. Because each language holds the key to fullest participation in each world, bilingualism is highly valued. No student regretted knowing either language, except as mastering English may have been accomplished at the expense of the vernacular. Many claimed one or the other as their primary language; all acknowledged the difficulty of learning Tewa or Keres as adolescents if they had not grown up knowing it as children.

Perhaps the thorniest dual-world elements to manage are those relating to individual and community good and to individualism and equality. These overlapping pairs together create a picture of opposing claims. When students contrast these terms, they say that they practice "independence" in the non-Indian world, and "unity" in the Indian world; at home "when you do something, it is for other people, and over here [at school] it is for yourself"; in the outside world, "to get somewhere, you have to be a success ... everyone's out trying to go on top of each other, [but] in the Pueblo world, there it's like really everyone's equal."

At the heart of these so-defined polar behaviors is school conduct. A senior girl says: "In school, I feel that I am always working to be better than the other person. This attitude that I perceive as an aggressive individual is one of the main differences between the Indian and non-Indian values." A Pueblo teacher reinforces this view: "In school, teachers tell them [students] that they have to be aggressive if you are going to get a job, maintain a job, be successful. Then, you have to speak your mind and stand up for what you think is right. At home, there are situations where you have to accept certain decisions, and you have to accept things."

School standards—competition, excelling, success, pride in succeeding, publicly proclaimed success—run counter to Pueblo ideals that have meaning well beyond lip service. I always wonder if ideals are more than empty words, reassuring perhaps of worthiness, but unable to withstand close scrutiny. I learned about the implications of their ideals when I asked a Pueblo educator to react to a quotation I'd found to the effect that in their traditional life, Pueblo people did not favor individual achievement. My respondent spoke at length. The matter of individual achievement, she said:

> actually strikes me at the core of my being. It truly is a dominant part of our lives. We were not verbally told that we should not ever be better than someone else, it was just understood, I suppose, through the way our parents behaved and the way the community behaved. A definite word comes to mind when I think about this situation. It's the Tewa word *showa*. *Showa* is a show-off, or someone who is proud. It's applied to anyone not behaving in what's considered good Pueblo

form. You know, when you're proud, you're putting on airs, you're misbehaving. When that term was applied, it was always meant to be derogatory. It's used to make sure that your behavior's always kept in check.

It applies to children and adults. If you had something, or you were quicker or brighter or braver or whatever, you didn't need to show it. You made sure that you [acted as if you] were equal to everyone else. Other people could acknowledge that you had a special talent, but you could never acknowledge that.

You know, to this day, if someone is boastful or tells me how good they are at something, I immediately begin to wonder what's wrong with them. The other impact that it's had on my life is just enormous. If I receive any kind of public attention, I start squirming.

This speaker added one more line, a telling thought given my focus on adolescents: "I'm not sure that as Pueblo people we have a good understanding of that [the points made above] until we're older." Students, accordingly, could well have trouble making sense of how success is defined at school and at home; of the acceptability of shining at school and of appearing like everyone else at home; and of optimizing personal gains at school and communal gain at home.

Indeed, a student aptly conveyed this very point in response to my question that asked if people in each world had different views of success. Her response: "I'm not sure the Indians even think about being successful. But the younger ones now want to go out and be successful. Older people express those words that you should make something of yourself, but I am not sure what success is in the Indian world." By this she means, I believe, not that she is uncertain or dubious about what is right to do at home, but that *success* is not a fitting word to describe what one does there. Yet success has most definitely entered the vocabulary of Indian youth and adults. The concept, the striving, the outcome—all are present in their lives, and all are symptomatic of the intrusion of non-Pueblo values of becoming.

Several additional elements, by no means exhausting the possibilities, will complete my examination of duality. One relates to the nature of time, often a matter of joking discussion among Pueblo people, when they refer to "Indian time," in contrast to "Anglo time." A student commented: "In the non-Indian world I am constantly pushed to do things at a certain time. I have to get to my first class on time. Eat lunch after fifth period and before sixth. We all have time limits when things are done in a non-Indian way. In the Indian way we do things when we think they should be done. There are no times set on when we do things. We work during the day until the sun sets to the West." I heard and read many such statements, some a bit more sophisticated in their reference to Anglo time as linear versus the Pueblo's as circular, but this student's words fairly contain what is most commonly stated. Since each world conceives time differently, students need to learn different modes of responding to the events of each world, another simplification, another dichotomizing, that by ignoring the commonalities, more sharply accentuates the differences.

Sharply accentuated differences also appear in the final pair of elements, which pit Pueblo patience, harmony, and cooperation against Anglo aggressiveness, exploitation, and competition. The behaviors in each of these sets apply to perceived dual-world contradictions about the earth, social relationships, presentation of self, conduct at school, and the like. At home, says a student, "if you speak your own mind, you get into trouble. Sometimes you get in trouble [there] doing what I do that is OK here [at school]." He believes that he has learned a school-based—and, by extension, an outside world-based—behavior: "Learn to be aggressive, so people will know where I stand. Speaking up ... is what this world is like." In the students' fantasy, patience, harmony, and cooperation create a gentle, nurturant Pueblo world, whereas aggressiveness, exploitation, and competition create a jarring, insecure, non-Indian world.

"Do you feel like you live in two worlds?" I ask a student. "Yeah," he answers, "because there is my religion part and the white part which, like, you go to school and get a job." Two parts, two worlds apart, two places of memory.

"What is there about your mom that you admire so much?" I ask another student. "The way she raised us," she answers. "How is that?" "Both worlds." "Both worlds?" "Yeah, we're living in the Indian ways and living in ... trying to be part of the white world." Inclined at first to present a parallel structure—"living in the Indian ways and living in ..."—she stops herself and shifts to "trying to be," words that capture a distinction between where her life is anchored, on the one hand, and where her life is aspiring, on the other.

A third student conveys the anguish this distinction creates:

> The younger people ... they will listen to their grandparents. They have been told by them that their culture is so important [and] when we are gone, you will have to keep it alive. What they [younger people] don't know is how to balance it out. The difference between the two worlds—they can't balance it, they have trouble living with it. You have a responsibility to participate in your Pueblo's religion. You have to carry it on. I guess it is just a constant struggle as to where should I be right now, what is most important, what should I be doing?

This student's closing thoughts about behavior for "right now" reflect the dilemmas of young students throughout their school days, but most particularly as they approach graduation's moment of decision. Indian High School students join their fellows nationwide at this crossroads, relieved to be done and anxiously anticipating next steps. But they part from their peers in a most conspicuous way, as the student above has observed. The earnest request to be an agent of cultural perpetuation pulsates through Pueblo life—"your Pueblo's religion, you have to carry it on." To succeed in school and the outside world is the corollary request, and if it is less insistently, deeply the object of socialization, it still reaps the advantage of approval from both the Indian and non-Indian worlds.

Though driven by the commands of contrary worlds, students do not predictably accept either. During their school years, Pueblo students will do what all American students do: attend class, make friends, love lunch time and holidays, fret over exams, and hope they fit in with and are accepted by peers and teachers. Their years of education in the whiteman's school can appear, on the face of it, misleadingly normal. Pueblo students, unlike other American students, however, will most predictably experience modest academic success.

5

"Go Have Yourself
a Good Education":
The Limits to Getting One

There's new and advanced technology out there—computers, and this and that. You have to go have yourself a good education. It is very important. You have to have a good job. You know, my grandpa would tell us to go to school. But he always says, "Don't you ever go and lose your Indian way."

—*Pueblo elder*

What I learn about the academic side of student life sometimes reassures me, sometimes does not. On the reassuring side, Indian High School teachers report that senior students' writing skills, ranked against national norms, place them 3 on a scale of 1 to 5. Furthermore, half or so of the students score at the 50th percentile on the California Test of Basic Skills, and their scores improve gradually from year to year. Furthermore, the students themselves report attributes of their school that suggest a place of decent teacher standards. In 1989, for example, 193 Indian High School students provided data for Table 5.1 (collected originally for an Effective Schools Project):

Current students verify that their teachers encourage them to work hard, care about them, and are supportive. This squares with my observations of the teachers at work. Moreover, teachers generally understand the cultural attributes that distinguish their students from non-Indian students and the instructional implications of those attributes. They discuss the implications and take account of them when they teach. Of course, they could be wiser, more accomplished, more resourceful; all teachers could. If all Indian High School teachers were as effective as the very best of them, I claim that the achievement problem I discuss in this chapter would remain.

TABLE 5.1

Student Perceptions of School Attributes

	Strongly Disagree	Disagree	Agree	Strongly Agree	Don't Know
Teachers in this school stress academic achievement.	1	6	58	30	5
Academic classes are generally challenging or difficult.	4	20	55	16	5
Teachers expect me to get good grades.	1	6	48	41	4
School encourages me to want to learn.	3	7	49	36	4
Teachers treat students as if they can learn.	3	9	57	26	5

Note. Numbers are percentages; $n = 193$.

Parents also encourage their children: "Every parent tells their kid that there is a time for fun, and what my dad tells us is to set our priorities right away." Not all parents offer steady, certain inspiration for their children, but the message the young people receive is "Schooling is important." At best, students confirm this message: "School means to me my life ... well, my ticket into the new world. Or into the real world, I should say. That is what school means to me. [She laughs as she thinks about what she just said.] I got butterflies now. I just got that feeling; I just got a chill."

This student's sentiments do not typically translate into academic achievement. This is the unreassuring side. Statewide student scores on New Mexico's 1989 High School Competency Exam placed Indian students last in reading, English, and mathematics, and next to last in science and social studies, just ahead of African American students.

Indian High School teachers and students provide evidence not of student inability but of disappointment at their level of academic success. Indian and non-Indian teachers alike agree that students are bright and capable, and that they want degrees and good careers. They lament that students do not pursue what they appear to value. Moreover, the students puzzle teachers: "I don't see that these kids come in with any serious language problems or serious academic problems, but over and over in talking with [fellow] teachers and [from] my own classroom observations is this failure [of students] to see that their hard work will get them anything."

This telling observation says, "Why work hard if I do not see that doing so will likely lead to results I desire?"

STUDENT EXPLANATIONS OF THEIR LIMITED ACADEMIC ACHIEVEMENT

A.P.:   You have the will power [as she had just told me] to listen to your grandpa and to do what he says, and to do it well.

S.:   Yep.

A.P.:   Why not at school?

S.:   I don't know. I guess I just don't try hard enough. I know I can do it, but I just get involved with my friends.

A.P.:   You know that you could do it, you could get really good grades.

S.:   But that is not happening.

A.P.:   That is not happening. Does that bother you at all?

S.:   Now that I think about it, it does. [She laughs.] I had never thought of it that way....

A.P.:   What advice would you give her [a hypothetical daughter who is attending Indian High School] to succeed at school?

S.:   Just to stay in school and not to use drugs, not to get in trouble, and to finish school.

A.P.:   What you have just said is very good for just getting by. But let's say you don't want her just to get by. You know what I mean? You want her to do really good here.

S.:   Uh huh. I don't know what I would tell her.

To learn how they would characterize their own academic performance, I interviewed forty students, the group I referred to earlier. I asked them how they thought they were doing, if they were doing as well as they'd like to, if they could work harder, whether they should work harder, and, of particular interest to me, how they would account for the limited effort they invest in their work. Their answers fell into a clear pattern.

To my opening inquiry, "How are you doing in your classes?" students responded either with a grade point average—for example, 3.5 or 3.1, on a 4-point system, with 4 as A—or with some general, brief comment: "coming along," "pretty good," "average," "not that great." One student said he was "doing great. I'm up to 2.8, starting to reach for 3.0." He was the only one of the 40 who said "yes" in response to my follow-up inquiry, "Are you doing as well as you'd like?" All others, many with better grade point averages, gave a direct "no" or a qualified "not really," "I'm doing better than past years," or "I thought I could do better." I followed this with, "Could you work harder?" then "Should you work harder?" Overwhelmingly, the students responded "yes" to both questions.

These are the reactions of students who do not intend to quit school and who would not if they could. This, too, is the norm at Indian High School, as are the hoped-for outcomes of schooling—its utility for self and community. Students speak with ease of these outcomes, locating them in the advice, wishes, or success of a parent or another relative—"My parents want me to become a doctor." "Mom and dad did so well; it makes me want to do the same."—or in their own aspirations for what they'd like to become or to avoid. What they say, students anywhere could say. They have occupational aspirations—"the main thing that motivates me some nights when I have a lot of homework is about me becoming a lawyer. That kind of motivates me." They have dreams—"I want to be recognized. I want to be looked up to. I want more in life." They have personal desires to satisfy—"I think education would rather come first than anything else if you really want everything you want. If you want clothes, if you want shoes, if you want a big house: if you want it, you got to work." And they are moved by the unfortunate experience of peers:

S.: The people who drop out ... they will have, like, maybe two kids. They're young, maybe my age. My best friend, we used to be at elementary school together, she had a baby. Yeah, she was smart.

A.P.: It was not because she was dumb that she did those things?

S.: She had a lot of talents. Like, she could draw. She could, I mean, like be on the honor roll if she, like, really tried.

I invited students to inform me about the puzzle of students' limited academic achievement, looking for enlightenment from their thinking, rationalizing, denying, whatever, as it relates to this puzzle. Indeed, I had wondered if they, too, see it as a puzzle. Teachers did, I knew, and students did, too, I learned, though not one that is a common part of student-initiated talk around the school. Among themselves, they do not routinely deliberate on the discrepancy between how smart they believe they are and how poorly they perform; ordinarily, they are not perplexed and curious about why this is so. When I present this bit of darkness to them, I hear no resistance to the basic statement of the case: they and their fellow students do not do well, despite possessing the intelligence to do well. And I hear no pleasure in their reactions to my inquiry. There should be none; the topic is depressing. I feel rewarded, however, by their struggling efforts to find words to discuss what they have experienced but usually have not given voice to.

The students did not identify intelligence as a factor to explain their relative lack of success. This point emerged most strongly when I asked them to describe the work of fellow students who they thought were very successful, and also when I followed up by wondering if they thought they, too, could be as successful. They thought they could. They might hesitate before answering, perhaps uncomfortable with my invitation to speak well about themselves. In the end, they did not see themselves as deficient in intellectual capacity compared to those they knew to be successful. Here is one student's account of a friend's success: "She studies more. She does her work. She really wanted to learn and she went to summer programs and stuff." "Could you be such a success if you wanted to?" "I think I could." "So she's not smarter than you?" "No, not really." And here is another: "He knows when to have fun and he knows when to stop. He wants to learn a lot of things, and he's very aggressive about getting information." And a third: "Just by the willingness or the strength or the power to succeed in what he does. He works real hard. He's got good determination to get it done." This, in brief, is why students think the academically successful are successful. What follows is why students think success eludes them.

My preliminary questions are general; they follow from the previous questions noted above: How are you doing in school, and could you and should you work harder than you do? I ask, "Why don't you [or your fellow students] work harder?" Their reflections sometimes take them to particular events and persons outside the school. One student began her account of how she "got really down" with the death of her grandmother. After that, "everything started slipping and slipping, and my grades kept going down." Before she could recover, two young friends died. "Death kept coming around me, and I was just getting down." Another student, thinking of a smart boy she knew who wasn't doing well, related his fate to that of his parents who "don't really care." "It's just rubbing off on their son. He wants to do his best but his parents make fun of him. I guess because he tries to do his best. He tries to make his life better than the way his parents are living, I guess. He just gave up because nobody really cares for him and really pays attention to him."

Both accounts strike me as plausible. The students did not often resort to explanations that located the source of the problem outside of themselves. Pueblo students, like students everywhere, are subjected to distracting, unmotivating personal circumstances. They do not do well in such circumstances. More often, their disposition was to look inside, at themselves, and most fundamentally at whether they cared about schooling. A student who recently had attended an elite summer school program had a point of comparison that most students do not have. He saw the elite students as having "different morals, different values, different aspirations of themselves." About himself he thought, in contrast, "As long as I am happy, I am content, but I don't think I have to push myself to be making so many bucks a year." After working unusually hard all summer, he returned to Indian High School and worked the way he always had, a way that would not single him out from other capable students who got As and Bs. He worked with an intensity that is consistent with Indian High School norms. They gave him the latitude to do well to a certain extent but not as he would have performed if he had continued to work at his elite summer-school level.

The crux of student caring resides in their perception of the worth of schooling, of whether they see it as important or unimportant. Students base importance on friends, basketball, the pleasure of particular subjects, or the value of schooling for reaching further opportunity. What is important can change, as students mature, for example, or with circumstances that present some aspect of schooling in a specially appealing way. Importance, moreover, can be held superficially: one knows the right words, even believes them, but does not internalize the value. It can be held deeply, so that if one slips, one soon returns to success-inducing behavior, as in the case of the student who said she will join her friends in cutting class. They, however, will not make up the work they missed, whereas she will. It can be held in such a way that one operates with effort and commitment at one time, with reluctance at another. Seldom is it held in the way expressed by a student at another school I studied. He said that he always asks himself why he has to learn what he is learning. Mostly, he cannot see its purpose, but he takes it "just on faith" that he should persist and do well—which he does—even though he often sees no connection between what he is learning and what he thinks he will do at any time in his life. As an Anglo, he does not have another life defining him and calling him to return, serve, and participate.

"I really don't know," clarified a junior girl. "I wonder if I really want it [educational success]. Sometimes, I think I don't." Having thought this, she instantly remarked, "But I do want it and I don't know why." In short, she is ambivalent. She could not have reached her 16th birthday without having heard the constant drumbeat of "education is good, education is important." Hearing the drumbeat, accepting the wisdom of its message, does not mean that it penetrates her understanding of the relationship between education, self, and community in clear, unambiguous terms. Thus she wavers, as her words above so clearly convey. That she wavers, that she has company in her wavering, and why are at the heart of my story. I will let one sophomore boy make the case:

A. P.:   Is doing well in school unimportant to you? Is it important?

S.:   I don't know. In a way, it's kind of important. It's kind of not too important in considering life and how people act. But it's really what people are doing for a living. It's kind of not mainly about life.

A.P.:   Going to school is not about life?

S.:   Huh, huh. It's mainly how you survive life.

Insight at such an abstract level is uncommon. More often, students were concrete. They accounted for working less hard than they thought they should and achieving at a lower level than they thought they could by their "laziness." Laziness translates into not feeling like doing the work, not getting around to the work, preferring to do something else, or getting too comfortable doing something to leave it to do school work. Students also invoked tiredness to account for their behavior. They felt too tired to work any more than they do, or they were too tired from the work they had done.

S.:   I think sometimes I just get tired.

A.P.:   Physically tired?

S.:   No, just mentally. Just, you know, you get bored or worn out. Not really with the school work or nothing, but just the thought. The whole idea, you know.

Students recognize aspects of school that demarcate it from their tribal community.[1] Such demarcations, discussed earlier in regard to dual-world contrasts, relate to competition in general, and include notions of success and striving to do well. At school, as one student said, "This world teaches you to be number one. You always have to be on top." School, he affirms, is a place where one is asked to push. "I could push myself, but at home you don't push yourself. You just take it easy. You live what you live. And I come here and, you know, it's difficult because you try to push yourself to do the work. And it's uneasy. It's uncomfortable." I don't believe that "just take it easy" means not working hard. The next thought, "You live what you live," better captures the Pueblo sense of the pace and intensity of work, of accepting what comes, recognizing the options one has, but appreciating that life is lived out in

---

[1]For further discussion of such discontinuities see Little Soldier (1985) and Mehan (1991).

accordance with a Grand Plan.

For students, the discontinuity between school and home is unresolved. Sensing different norms for how to be, they do not give each their due in a way that acknowledges, in effect, here is how I must think, be, and do in the one setting, and here is how in the other setting. They know that they do not sustain school-effective behavior. Such behavior is a prize just out of reach. "It's, like, growing up, I guess. [Students] don't really see competition, so they're not used to it, and they won't see it until once they get into school. Some people cannot adjust to it, so they give up." And from another student: "I feel I can do it [compete], but I'm just, it's just the thought of losing or not getting as far as I want. It makes me stop myself from trying to compete. People are scared of losing, and that's just why people just don't want to even start competing in the first place."

Declarations of schooling's value do not translate into persisting motivation to work. Can one work hard at something that is not about life, when just "the whole idea of it" wears you out? Students can articulate that school is about surviving, understood in material terms. As adolescents, they seldom are blessed with the breadth of insight into what school is or is not about as a fact that is conjoined within the responsibilities and opportunities of their individual *and* community life, and why, therefore, they may feel lazy or tired.

The students already have elaborated their attentiveness to learning in the instructional settings of their tribal community, and their relative inattentiveness at school. Their self-identified sense of laziness, weakness, and tiredness constitutes a malaise, "an indefinite feeling of generalized debility" (*Webster's Third New International*).[2] It does not seem farfetched to associate the students' malaise with alienation. Though the roots of tradition remain in place, they embrace insistently hard-to-achieve ideals. In addition, becoming a person of their second world is a seductive challenge, but the roots for so being are shallow, the necessity of its good so often seemingly at odds with Pueblo ideals.

The alienation, like some forms of anxiety, seems to be free-floating, located in the midst of what one may feel is uncertain and unclear in each world. It is experienced here and there, intermittently; it is generally more energy-sapping and disorganizing than disabling. Students are not devoid of the stabilizing effects of norms, direction, a sense of efficacy, meaning, and the like. But the challenges and confusions in their cultural duality rock these goods and set them

---

[2]In this regard, see Ogbu's observations of nonimmigrant minorities:

> [They] tend to equate schooling with one-way acculturation or assimilation into the dominant group ... Consequently, they do not behave in a manner that maximizes academic success. In fact, they are generally characterized by what may be called low-effort syndrome or lack of persevering academic effort. [Ogbu 1987:258]

trembling, so that their life course is now clear, now blurred, now operative, now hesitant. Ultimately, all Pueblo students know, as do all Pueblo adults, that within their communities only Pueblo ways have primacy. Community members who forsake their community may prosper in non-Indian terms, but theirs is not the success of the vaunted, complicated dual-world mastery, with its balance strongly tilted toward Pueblo orthodoxy. Alienation promises to exist as long as success in school and the other institutions of the whiteman's world bears the attribute of "possibly forbidden, uncertainly rewarding." This attribute taints both the success and those who achieve it, and chastens those who pursue it.

Students do advance other explanations of their limited achievement. They account for their own and others' behavior by reference to *sex*—"Like the boys, they don't want to show their smartness. They say, 'School is not my thing,'" and some girls think, "What use is it anyway? I'm just going to go back to the Pueblo and be pregnant"; to *teasing*—"Like if they do good, friends and stuff, you know, they tease them"; to *jealousy*—"Like when you get real good grades, people get jealous"; to *distraction*—"They're so involved in what their friends are doing" and "There is too much going on, like, around"; and to *negative peers*—"They're, like, involved with other people that don't do that good in school and they probably try not to do well."

What the students say here also seems plausible. Much that they said emerged after pauses and "I don't knows," and, at times, after uncomfortable silence and long deliberation. They were not glib. Answer they could, but not with ease, and seldom at length, even with time and encouraging probes. They did not like doing less well than they thought they could and working less hard than they thought they should. This problem was neither pleasant nor easy to discuss. I invited folk explanations in order to learn if and how students thought about the phenomenon of school achievement. Of course, nothing they said applies to every student. What strikes me as most fundamental for understanding the phenomenon is their characterization of student behavior that amounts to malaise, for now a proximate explanation, since the malaise has not yet been accounted for. In the last section of this chapter I will return to this point.

TEACHER EXPLANATIONS OF STUDENTS' LIMITED ACADEMIC ACHIEVEMENT

A.P.:   In general, do the students work hard?

T.:   I would say no, they are not working hard enough. I think that's what makes me angry. Why aren't they working hard? When teachers tell me that it's really the kids, it's hard for me to buy that because I feel very

strongly that if you as a teacher, you're committed, you set your expectations, and you stick with them, then they will rise to....

A.P.:   Is the difference between [students] working hard and not working hard
the teacher's skill?

T.:   It is a factor, one of the factors.

Other Indian High School teachers affirm this view, comfortable with the
charge that their classroom conduct is relevant to how their students work, but
unwilling to make their own conduct the sole or major factor of consequence.
That teachers and administrators can make a difference against odds that
ordinarily limit student performance we learn from bright spots in Hawaii and
elsewhere (for example, see Tharp 1994; Tharp and Gallimore 1989; John-Stei-
iner and Osterreich 1975). These successes are generally located in elementary,
less often in middle, uncommonly in secondary schools. Overall, they do not
abound. Under the conditions of my study, I cannot assess what different
outcomes might have resulted if teachers were other than they are.

Although teachers join students in identifying a number of factors, they do
not label students as lazy. Unanimous in believing that students generally do
not work hard enough, and, often, that students unrealistically think they do
work hard, teachers see students as too often not persisting, lacking the desire
to work, preferring to do other things, and tired—all of which amounts to
teacher verification of the students' malaise.

They are aware of the students' self-attribution of laziness, and that the
school's report card may unwittingly support the claim by having "lazy" as one
of the codes teachers can check to describe student behavior. But, generally,
they prefer explanations that accuse neither students nor themselves. As individual or general explanatory factors, teachers speak of *dysfunctional home
conditions*—"There's something happening at home, or something that has
happened in the past that they [students] can't shake"; *historical circumstances*—"Indians have been considered to be at the bottom of the barrel
academically, carrying the lowest jobs, and I think that probably that attitude
has something to do with it"; *language complications*[3]—"I have some students
who are almost dominant in their own languages.... I see a lot of puzzled faces

---

[3]In a 1989 study, an Indian High School educator found that students whose first language is
their Indian vernacular are four times more likely to drop out of school than other students. I have
seen no further corroborating data of this powerful point, though Walker found that "speaking
[their] native language ... is also the source of many learning difficulties among Indian students"
(1972:3). The significance of sustaining competence in the Indian vernacular can not be over-
stated. Should that competence prove to be inversely correlated with staying in school, then a truly
complicated circumstance exists, for no Indian educator or lay person would want to give up either
language skill or school success.

... translating is going on. I see that and I know that. I went through that"; *peer pressure*—"She [a student] doesn't want to excel because that would bring attention to her, which she does not want. She never wants to be in the limelight. She says, 'I just want to do something I can turn in, and get it done and get by'"; *past schooling*—"They come in [to Indian High School] with patterns of 'If I shut up, if I don't ask questions, if I don't raise my hand, she [the teacher] will leave me alone and I can get by with the minimum.' That is the pervasive attitude." "Is it the BIA [Bureau of Indian Affairs] system?" "No. [According to school records], in 3 recent years, graduating seniors came to this school from 76 different schools!"; and *present schooling*—Teachers felt that by oversupporting and overnurturing students, they hindered their learning from adversity and becoming independent. Caring too much becomes an unintended obstacle to academic success as students grow accustomed to an omnipresent helping hand, always being given a second chance, with no sure price paid for poor work or late work. Students confirm this point: "It's, like, you have everything done for you. Like, if you're not passing, your teachers and everybody that's involved will all get together.... So, OK, they're being real lenient on you. It's OK to a certain point. Then they help you too much, and then when you kind of get dependent, we know we can slack off and you know they will help you."

Teachers offer different explanations from students'. They are less troubled by thinking about the matter of student academic success, and more practiced in doing so. Periodically, at workshops and meetings, they discuss the matter; most often they see students' low self-esteem as the explanatory culprit. Low self-esteem is a shorthand way of speaking about the nonpersisting, tired, unmotivated student behavior that they and the students agree exists.

From the vantage of their sophistication, teachers also saw explanatory possibilities in nonschool factors, particularly the students' cultural life. On the one hand, say Pueblo teachers, students may see a marked irrelevance in school learning as it relates to what they value and aspire to at home: "I have had friends who would just rebel against school and schoolwork, and yet be somebody responsible and respectable in their community. I have had friends who really struggled through school and then go back and be governor or an official." This school-failure-community-success distinction is one I often heard, as if to reassure that achievement of note occurs in more than one arena, and school success is not the ultimate triumph. On the other, students may be torn by their sense of the impact of schooling on their tribal traditions: "Some of the message I have gotten from the kids' behavior is they are simultaneously afraid to fail or succeed. I think that part of the fear of success is that they will be driven farther away from their culture." This is part of the students' dual-world tug-of-war. Being "afraid to fail or succeed" undermines student will. As they progress through school, doubt may win out. It is a formidable disincentive.

MY EXPLANATION OF STUDENTS' LIMITED
ACADEMIC ACHIEVEMENT

> Tom says the teacher told him at school that the only way white people will ever get to look up to Indian people as equals ... is for us to *prove* we're equal.
>
> *—Pueblo youth, speaking to Coles (1977:410)*

> Someday, you'll be governor of your tribe.
>
> *—Pueblo principal, addressing students*
> *at a grade school graduation ceremony*

> Sometimes I like them, but then I remind myself that I should watch every white man I see very carefully!
>
> *—Pueblo youth, speaking to Coles (1977:426)*

Imagine waking thoughts that alternate between a discomforting world in which one must prove one's worth for no reason other than one is Indian, and a comforting world in which because one is Indian, one could be governor of his tribe. Imagine thinking that though the school one attends is tied to the world of self-proving, the results of having attended this school are typically not sure, clear, or convincing. Imagine further thinking not only that the school is disconnected from the traditional world of the governor, but that its outcomes may be harmful to that world. Imagine finally thinking that every word of every elder, every word of any authority, argues for the desirability of attending school, while the accumulated experiences of one's eyes, ears, and being often argue to the contrary.

On the face of it, schooling is valuable. To be sure, incompetent educators and indifferent parents and communities may obscure and negate the value of schooling for individual, community, and societal well-being. When incompetence and indifference are not prevailing facts of consequence, how can we account for student malaise, for their inability to persist as learners in school?

Student and teacher explanations clarify a basic fact: there are many reasons why any particular student will not prosper in school, and what affects one student negatively will not predictably affect other students the same way. Indeed, what undermines one student may well motivate and challenge another. Some observers offer the awful historical legacy of schooling as explanation, noting that many Indians endured an era of schooling based on "ethnocide" (see Chadwick 1972; Collier 1988; and Grobsmith 1981), that is, on the destruction of Indian culture. In a nationwide study of Indian groups, Fuchs and Havighurst identified five negative factors: the students' low socioeconomic status, the limited schooling of their parents, language deficiencies (because English often was not their home language), cultural discontinuities between home and school, and, more generally, the duality of their lives (1972:123–135). None of these factors can be ruled out.

More than 50 years ago, a scholar of Pueblo life observed, "The American school does not mean much to the Indian child; his home, his pueblo do" (White 1942:57). As I see it, this is a decisive truth to consider for understanding the school behavior of Pueblo youth. Where is the weight of memory located? A Pueblo son says, "If it all boiled down to giving up a portion of my life, I would choose to give up the non-Indian part." And a Pueblo leader exults, "The community knows who I am, knows who my family is. Knowing that you have been recognized within the community that you call home—I don't think that anyone would give that up for anything else in the world. There are no substitutions any way that you look at it."

The Pueblo ideal invites its adherents to feel a deep sense of obligation and affection for their tribal community. An individual's destiny is tied, possibly inextricably, to the tribal home. Traditional religious commitments can be enacted in but one place. One can pray anywhere; only at home can the religious experience be consummated, because it requires one's tribal group. One can take up residence anywhere; only at one's Pueblo can one find one's Indian home and community.

For Pueblo people, the outside world contains no counterpart to their tribal community. Pueblo communities are not just like small places of residence, such as the nation's many villages, that have the capacity to attach their residents in a profound way. They are not just like settlements of religious nationals or religious-ethnic groups, such as city neighborhoods of Italian Catholics or Russian Jews, that can provide meaning and belonging to people of common ancestry, religion, and history. They are not just like people of a particular regional occupation or geographic enclave, such as people in a fishing village or mountain hollow, whose lives are shaped by particular ways of making a living or by the shared isolation in a striking configuration of land and water. Pueblo tribes possess all these attributes. They are, as well, tiny, "sovereign," theocratic nation states, with laws of succession to insure continuity of secular and sacred leadership.

Indian leaders of an earlier day rejected schools because in them their children became "good for nothing" (*Between Two Milestones* 1972:78). In current versions of those schools, that harsh judgment is much less warranted. Still, it is far from clear what, in Pueblo terms, schooling enables children to be good for, and whether the forthcoming good is worth the price paid in exchange. Young and old Pueblo people know what they are good for at home; it is part of everyone's socialization. An Indian High School staff worker remarked that the students she sees at school are just kids in their limited role as students, whereas the same students at home are important, playing roles that contribute to community life.

Perhaps most persuasive of the value of what students learn at home is their comparative assessment of those who instruct them at school and at home. When I thought of "teachers" in the service of learning in school and community, I imagined students listening in both settings. Accordingly, I asked students to describe themselves as listening learners at home and school. They had never thought of this before; when they did, they surprised themselves and me. With few exceptions, they said that they listened intently to grandparents, or to whoever else in their family played an instructional role (for example, a godparent, an aunt, or an uncle); occasionally, they listened to a teacher, counselor, or staff member in the same way. They overwhelmingly concluded that they were seriously attentive both comparatively and absolutely at home, but not, they realized, at school. *It was as if a different person were present in each setting.* They unhesitatingly accounted for the difference.

To begin with, the notion of respect for elders is basically intact. For their instructional purposes, Pueblo home teachers are honored. Such respect does not predictably extend to anyone outside of tribal boundaries, including Pueblo school teachers. Beyond respect, students were convinced that their home teachers knew what was true and worth knowing, that is, what they needed to learn to live as a good Pueblo person, both now and as an adult.

How do you listen when your grandparents talk to you or when you are in the *kiva*? "With all my heart and everything I have," answered one student, in an epiphany of intensity and commitment. Students could not imagine listening so devotedly at school: "You listen for a while and then you get side-tracked because it is not that important to you." "I listen to my teachers," another student explained, "but it's not the same thing because they're talking about homework, and do this and do that." I could chalk up to hyperbole the students' school–home contrasts, to needing to support the beleaguered home team, but my evidence points otherwise. It is clear from the following four voices that what students are contrasting in each setting is *who* is instructing them about *what*:

> At the *kiva*, you have to listen more; you can't mess around. You have to have a clear mind. You are going into there for religion. You have to pay more attention. And at school, you know, you can mess around.

> You know, sometimes you go into the classroom with a clear mind as much as you can. And you sit there and you pay as much attention as you can. I did that

at the beginning of this year. And the more and more I sat there and I tried to listen, the more it just came that I was bored with it.

In the *kiva*, you know, you don't really have that much people to talk to. You don't have your friends to mess around with. And, second of all, you know, you always gotta have your mind clear as much as you can. ["So the same guy in these two places and he's different in each place?" I ask.] Yeah, I don't know how to explain that. That's it, you know. Religion I will pay attention to, because that is my main root I came from. And then with the school, you know, I will pay attention, but sometimes I won't be there, you know. So, I always listen more at home than I would listen up here. My religion, where I came from, my roots come first. And then comes school.

You listen when you're in class, but not in the same way. It's just like it's different somehow.

Awareness of what is "different somehow" was brought consciously to students' minds by my inquiries, which were, of course, not intended to create any sense of differences, but, rather, to learn if they existed, and what might underlie them if they did. Students are told repeatedly to respect their school teachers, and they freely acknowledge the propriety of doing so. But at school "it's like they can only tell you so much. At home, you have to do it. You can't say, 'OK, *maybe* I will.'" Pueblo students believe that teaching and learning at school and community not only occur in physically separate places, but also are truly separate processes, as epitomized in a student's reflection on each setting: "With school, basically, all you have to do is try. You don't have to feel it in your heart." His words are revealing: learning accomplished by trying and learning that requires feeling—these distinctions are outside the normal realm of what teachers are taught to do and what they consider they need to do as educators. Community legitimation graces both Pueblo tribal instructors and the contents of their instruction; their school counterparts enjoy no comparable endorsement. Moreover, school learning lacks the emotional bond that for Pueblo learning is a condition for effective mastery. If how one feels about what one is learning establishes a necessary condition for learning, then the circumstances for learning, and its outcomes, are marked as special.

What is special about the Pueblos occurs within a continuing history of racism, prejudice, hostility, and affront in the outside world. Students spoke of being "tired of people calling us savages just because we don't have nice clothes and a lot of money like them"; of attending a school where "the whites were always putting us down"; and of going into a store and first being ignored and then treated poorly by its employees. One Pueblo man shamefully recalls his experience as a young boy living in the city. When his very Indian-looking grandmother came to visit the family, he refused to meet her at the bus "because

I didn't want the other neighborhood kids to see me. I guess when you're young, you have that sense of at least I can hide I'm Indian." Another recalls, also with shame, playing cowboys and Indians as a child, and wanting most to be a cowboy. In his experience, cowboys always won. And a Pueblo woman contrasts being at home, where she is "not continually being challenged as to who I am," with being away, where "I don't want to say this, but sometimes they make you feel like you're just some dumb Indian sitting there." Finally, an Indian High School teacher observes that when she takes students away from school for a competition with non-Indian students, "I always need to reinforce, 'Come on, you guys, these kids are just like you. Let's go beat them. Let's not be intimidated by them.'" And beat them they might, while suffering lingering doubt about whether they really are just like them, and, moreover, whether they shouldn't be intimidated.

Schooling is necessary to become competent in the very world that Pueblo people perceive as rejecting them. In reaction to this world, students are angry, fearful, and resentful. "When I was little I used to think, 'God, I wish they [white people] would go back [to Europe].' I used to dream that I would make a time machine to go back [to Columbus's arrival] and give those Indians some machine guns and shoot them away." Some want most to be left alone to live their lives apart from external demands and necessities. Some "want to go out there and prove to the people who have stereotyped us that all Indians are not drunks and live on welfare." Some have self-doubt, a feeling of inferiority, "because people never have high expectations of Native Americans." This I hear from an Indian teacher when speaking about her Pueblo students, and, as I eventually learn, when speaking about herself.[4] The waters of opportunity in the non-Indian world contain both pearls and sharks.

Navigating these waters benefits from advice-giving family members who mean well, wish the best for their children, and exhort extensively. Too often, however, theirs are the words of people who have neither done well in school nor used the outcomes of schooling to particular advantage.[5] Students know that these family members mean what they say, but "Some of them, they tell me, you know, not to do all that what they did, you know, like, so I won't make the same mistakes as they did." Perhaps most telling is a dearth of persons who

---

[4]Wax, Wax, and Dumont approvingly cite a study of 112 Indian students from over a period of 33 years that related high college dropout rates to poor preparation and "the psychological attitudes of the Indian, e.g., 'inferiority complex'" (1964: 9–10). The study is by W. W. Ludeman (1960).

[5]On the parental role in their child's school success, Ogbu writes: "Although black parents verbally stress the importance of education ...they also convey to the children subtly and unknowingly contradictory messages powerful enough to cancel out much of their educational encouragement and efforts" (Ogbu 1987:266).

have done well in school and with school, as well as with tribal commitments, of persons, in short, who model dual-world success.

Regrettably, the landscape of Pueblo life abounds with counter-examples; students hear encouraging words, but may live with discouraged people. For example, the girls speak of sisters and cousins and aunts who graduated from high school, went to college, and came home after a semester or two: "One had a baby early and the other, she just quit and didn't do nothing else." The boys speak comparably of brothers and cousins and uncles: "He was, like, a honor roll student all the way in high school. Then, when he went to college, he never made his first semester. He just dropped out. He said he tried, but I figure, you know, there was a thing." The thing was drinking, a way out of an unresolved, if not seemingly unresolvable, personal and communal issue. An abundance of such examples is instructive; an abundance of exhorting words to the contrary struggles to overcome the debilitating effects of the examples.

The net result of the negative examples is an unplanned, unwanted effect that itself becomes a cause: numbers of relatives, friends, and neighbors who could have done well in high school, but didn't, and numbers who did well in high school, but later failed or underachieved after receiving further education. This subgroup establishes a standard for how to behave in school and for how to use schooling; by its size and normality, it legitimates educational underuse and failure. An Indian High School teacher describes what she has observed:

> We had a person from the Native American Scholarship Association speak, and she kept repeating, "Sixty or seventy percent is the dropout rate from college for Native Americans." Before the first semester, I think it was. When someone else comes in and tells them about it they listen, and it is depressing for them. That makes them shaky. I can see the look in their eyes. They have this underlying, "You're going to fail, you're going to fail. You're going to be one of the great percentages." We encourage them, but in the back of their minds they just hear it over and over: "Such a great number of Native Americans have failed. You aren't going to do what you want to do. You are going to end up working with minimum wage."

"A part of me," says a Pueblo mother, "feels the pain of saying, 'Young people, you *have* to work hard, you *have* to become educated, because you are my future.'" Unable to imagine thinking otherwise, she joins the mass of Pueblo parents, elders, and leaders who urge, extol, and motivate on behalf of schooling's benefits. "Sometimes," responds a student, "you just get used to hearing that, and it goes in one ear and out the other. 'Work hard, try better, you can do it, you are smarter than that, and stuff like that.' It's just, like, work, work, work." A fellow student concludes, "It is a lot easier just to let everything go."

"In this world," writes a student, "there is always a maze you have to take or a door you have to find so you can get out! to succeed! In the Indian world it is peaceful." From the attractions and necessities of each world, Pueblo students experience a tug-of-war and resulting confusion.[6] As if following a script, students spoke repeatedly of the confusion that results from this tug-of-war.[7] This is how they identified their state of mind. Even when they clearly grasped the impossibility of reconciling competing claims, they could not count on understanding and support, as they defined it, from both school and home: "The hardest part is when my elders say that I am not doing what I am supposed to do because of the non-Indian world, and the same thing is told to me by the people at work and school. This is the most discouraging to me because these two worlds are very important to me." A student expressed the sense of struggle most poignantly: "I am struggling to know my Pueblo language. I feel that I will lose because I am in a point in life where I have to go on with my education. I am pulled by a huge chain by the white world, while being pulled by a cheap cotton string [by the Indian world]. Sometimes, it's so confusing and depressing I don't know what to do." The "cheap cotton string" does not reflect the student's scorn for his Pueblo, but, rather, the relatively more powerful means of the white world to have its way in his life. When it does, he says sadly, "I will lose." Pueblo adults confirmed that they, too, have occasion for struggle: "In my head, it is a tug-of-war, a constant pushing and pulling." A teacher explained that he experiences

> two nations pulling you left and right and you are in the middle. You are obligated one way because you are a citizen of the United States, and you are also coming from another nation with its own sovereignty. Like the feast right now. I myself get in a bind of should I miss work and attend that or should I stay here and fulfill my duties. Not only do I have a duty here, but I have a duty there. Once I obtained my degree I really felt a sense of relief. I made it. [He pauses.] [But] no, I'm not settled yet.

Quite possibly, he never will settle this "two nations" issue, in the sense of resolving it, though he may work out a tolerable form of accommodation. Given his values, resolution by his own doing is unlikely because it involves clarifying that which affects individuals but actually is communal in nature, and thus

---

[6]For a contrasting outcome, see Bruner's account of the Mandan-Hidatsa. When they "are with Whites they act one way, and when they are with Indians in another. This situational role specificity has become a perfectly natural routine procedure. It is not a source of confusion" (1961:267).

[7]On the point of a tug-of-war and confusion, see Blanchard (1983:118) and Joe (1994: 108–9).

requires clarification, elaboration, and sanctification by the tribal keepers of tradition. Only they are authorized to interpret and sustain its meanings. Only they can establish the terms of an accommodation that involves "the maintenance of cultural integrity as well as the movement to become an integral part of a larger societal framework" (Berry 1980:13).

Matters of community survival and the sacred can appear as colliding alternatives to pursuits associated with the outside world. Alternatives parade as either-or choices that cloud the prospects of one's life. Student thinking reflects this perception. The following voices have a crowd of supporters:

> Sometimes it gets very confusing and frustrating to choose between the worlds. It is frustrating because you have to give up something else to have the other one.

> As a native American I feel like I can't really learn my culture because to me the White culture seems to be more dominant and if I start to learn my Native culture like the old people, I will fall behind in the dominant world. But at the same time, I want to learn my culture.

Students experience clashing necessities, uncertain how to "weigh and balance" and thereby manage what appears to be ever in conflict—the responsibilities, opportunities, and expectations of each world. Joseph Suina (Cochiti) writes: "One day I dozed off in class after a sacred all-night ceremony. I was startled awake by a sharp jerk on my ear, and informed coldly, 'That ought to teach you to attend "those things" again.' Later, all alone, I cried. I couldn't understand why or what I was caught up in. I was receiving two very different messages; both were intended for my welfare" (1985:35). Suina recalls a time several decades ago when schools were more fully disagreeable places for Indian children and for "those things" of tradition in their lives. Are the outcomes different today, even granted that teachers and policies have changed, particularly at Indian High School? A student muses on the relative importance of what she learns at school and at home:

> Home learning more important than school? I think it is equal. It is questions like this that are kind of pulling you apart, and you don't really know how to answer them. We never really thought of it, and now that this question came up, I feel like it is there and it feels funny. There are two different ways. I think they are both equally important, yes, but then your number one priority would be home.

As students speak and write about their lives, they repeatedly represent the tug, sometimes more an undertow, of their duality in the seemingly contradictory language of equality—"both are equally important, yes," and of salience—"but then your number-one priority would be home." The logical impossibility of the behavior implied by this language belies the nonlinear ways that we live our lives—now observing equality, now acknowledging salience—in no necessarily predictable order or circumstance. Possibly she lives in accord with her two stated predispositions, uncompelled to establish a consistent pattern, though by not doing so she may eventually abandon one or the other predisposition or vacillate between them in a personally upsetting manner.[8]

A Pueblo educator reflected on this matter: "I often feel like it is hard not to give the kids a double message: stay at home and be involved and go get the best education that you possibly can." The occasion for his reflection is a forthcoming feast day at one of the Pueblos: "So there is a big conflict, a struggle. Even if you have that student here, she is thinking about what is going on at home. She is not really here, maybe physically; mentally, she is at home. That is what I see." This educator's double message is like the classic double bind, but not completely. In the logical contradictions of the double bind, if one side wins, the other side must lose. Fearing wrath from those in the direction not taken, or otherwise unable to make a choice, one moves in neither direction, thereby avoiding both the rewards and punishments forthcoming from each. The internal costs from this avoidance are another matter. Some Pueblo persons may see their cultural alternatives in terms that translate into the zero-sum pangs of the double bind.

I think otherwise. In what the teacher sees as "Two nations pulling you left and right," and the student as "two different ways," are circumstances that fall short of the double bind's strict oppositions. Pueblo youth affiliate with their sacred tribal home, learning that they must put their tribal community first. Their antagonism, sometimes revulsion, toward the outside world combines with the negations of a large Pueblo subgroup of educational underuse and failure. Students become alternately fearful and optimistic about living with and living without the whiteman's school. If they do well in such an institution, they will hear: "On the one hand, [Pueblo] people admire you and hold you up as an example. On the other, they can also say very unkind things about you, and make sure that you know it and feel it." Together, these circumstances transform the whiteman's school into an ambiguous ("admitting of two or more meanings" [*Webster's Third International Dictonary*]) institution that creates feelings of ambivalence ("contradictory emotional or psychological attitudes"

---

[8]For a useful psychodynamic picture of the complications of identity development under conditions of duality, see DeVos and Suárez-Orozco (1990:229–36). De Vos relates one aspect of the adolescent developmental model drawn from Phinney (in DeVos and Suárez-Orozco 1990: 231–2) to school success: "Quick foreclosure" of adolescent identity can lead to "an exclusionary defense that interferes with school education among some ethnic minorities" (DeVos and Suárez-Orozco1990:232).

[*Webster's Third International Dictionary*]).[9] In such a school, students will be irresolute, moved as they are by the claims of approach and avoidance.

If Pueblo people cared less than they do about their Pueblo life and if they needed less the acculturating outcomes of the school, their lives would be simpler, less driven by ambiguity, less perplexed by the joustings of an inside and outside world. But when what they persist in caring about and can't escape needing are at odds, then they are like people climbing a ladder that more or less simultaneously goes up and down. This creates an illusion of movement, but does not get anywhere.

In this situation of ambiguity and ambivalence,[10] one avoids the paralysis of the true double bind by responding sometimes to each world, sometimes to one or the other world, but tentatively, half-heartedly, lacking conviction. This is the response of people who hear repeatedly about the necessity of something, but are not decisively convinced of it. Or they can't see how acting on the necessity is congruent with other necessities that they value more or understand better. The institutions and outcomes of cultural becoming rest awkwardly in Pueblo life, which entails no shortage of ambiguities and ambivalences of its own. Yet the most probable escape from the dire double bind is the Pueblos' continuing allegiance and affection for community and family. If tossed by confusion, they seldom doubt where home is.

Because the school is fundamentally an ambiguous institution, ambivalence[11] runs deep. Teachers are ambivalent about their capacity to Indianize Indian High School, many about the necessity of doing so. Although teachers and students accept the fact of Pueblo cultural duality, they are ambivalent about its meaning and how the school may respond to it. Teachers share student ambivalence about forms and degrees of academic success that may be dysfunctional in Pueblo communities. Students are ambivalent about school success, knowing that it may earn them disapproval from less successful peers and scorn from elders who see success as acting white. Elders are ambivalent about

---

[9]Erickson writes: "Caught in ambivalence between multiple cultural worlds, Alaskan native youth resist adopting the complete system of school-defined literacy, and then suffer the consequences of marginal acquisition. They do not belong fully to the old ways or to the new" (1984:539).

[10]For a useful discussion of sociological ambivalence, see Heilman (1977). He describes five types of such ambivalence, several of which appear to fit Pueblo people. For example, there is "ambivalence bred by contradictory cultural demands and values embedded in any given society" and "ambivalence [that is] indigenous to those who are forced to accept and adapt to the contradictory values attached to a plurality of contradictory cultures" (1977:228). For the original source of the concept, see Merton and Barber (1963).

[11]Ogbu speaks of ambivalence in the context of what he calls "secondary cultural differences," identifying an "ambivalent/oppositional cultural frame of reference" and an "ambivalent oppositional cultural/language identity" (1992:n.p.). He elaborates the point elsewhere (Ogbu 1991).

an institution that for most of their life was devoted to assimilation. Pueblo communities are ambivalent about the nature of the mandate they should provide for the conduct of Indian High School, less clear than they would like to be about what goals and what instructional forms should be primary.

In Pueblo society, schooling remains a phenomenon of surfaces. Unlike Catholicism (see Fox 1973:203–4, 275), it is an unassimilated good. Pueblos have never absorbed schooling into the lifeblood of their tribal culture, fitting it comfortably into place as one among many integrated elements of their cultural complex. As an unassimilated good, schooling's benefits are shrouded in uncertainty, so that the logic of striving for and attaining these benefits is not persuasive.[12] For Pueblo people, it is not so much the matter of the disillusioned "What's the use of trying?" (Ogbu 1986: 107) because I won't get anywhere even if I do succeed in school; this is the job-ceiling effect (Ogbu and Matute-Bianchi 1986: 117). It is the matter of the uprooting "What's the use of succeeding?" because if I do get anywhere, my tribe may no longer accept me, I may no longer fit in well, I may no longer feel as comfortably attached, and I may have complicated my life by the introduction of a continually competing alternative to the requirements of tribal participation.[13] Thus are schools ambiguous to Pueblo communities, and they will remain ambiguous until their ends and means are somehow integrated with Pueblo tribal life. Until then, Indian students undergo institutional and cultural dissonance.

---

[12]As a postscript, though not as a mere afterthought, I must clarify that modest academic achievement and the sense of schooling as a disturbingly unresolved factor in Pueblo life are not *notably* structured by sex or class. Indian High School, a coeducational boarding school, excluded no applicants for financial reasons (recall that the tuition of $50 each semester was overlooked, if necessary). It equally favored female and male students in its admission practice and in its provision of curricular and extracurricular opportunities and honors. Impressionistic data, my own and that of teachers, is that females tended to do better in school.

The insights students provided about their lives as students and as Pueblo members were not distinguishable by sex. Neither they nor Pueblo adults identified differences or complications that invited me to explore school effects by sex or class. To be sure, all of Pueblo life is shaped by role definitions that direct the lives of its people by age and sex. And in the course of tribal life, power more definitely accrues to males. Nevertheless, neither these facts nor the supposed benefit of having a close family member who did well at school, graduated from college, and got a good job, *necessarily* create the school as an experience that predictably means one thing or another to male and female students or to richer and poorer students.

In short, ambiguity, ambivalence, and malaise strike most Pueblo students, for the course of their life is headed toward a dual-world quandary that does *not* preclude satisfaction and accomplishment in each world but cloaks it in confusion, uncertainty, and irresolution. One's Pueblo tribal home and community is likely to benefit from this quandary because it is the place of primary socialization and membership and, therefore, of more certain reward.

[13]For the application of this point to other involuntary minority groups, see Ogbu and Matute-Bianchi's discussion of the "linear acculturation model" (1986: 98–9).

This is not the cultural discontinuity[14] that a host of researchers (for example, Au, Jordan, Jacob, Phillips, Tharp, and Suina) seek to overcome through culturally appropriate pedagogies. Theirs is the discontinuity of learning styles, as Vogt, Jordan, and Tharp elaborated (1987). It is life ways that I see at issue. Schools of the outside world promote accomplishment in that world. When they do, they are at odds with the ideals of Pueblo culture as currently conceived. It is not how to succeed in school but how to be accomplished in both worlds that remains a mystery. Who one can become in personal and vocational terms as a result of school success is not yet authorized by Pueblo tradition, not yet integrated in Pueblo social structures. So the charge of acting white is social control at its best: If you act white, you are not acting Indian. If you can't act white, then what is school good for? If you don't act Indian, you abandon your people. If you don't act Indian, then who are you? If you act both white and Indian, you invite both personal and communal strain and discomfort.

The school, as an institution of becoming, and the *kiva*, as an institution of remaining, are antagonistic, as are the cultures from which these parallel institutions arise. Some people do manage well with each institution and its cultural context, the result of luck or giftedness or resilience. They do not necessarily know how they achieved their success; most Indian High School students are unable to emulate them.

"A man makes his prayers; he sings his songs. He considers all that is important and special to him, his home, children, his language, the self that he is. He must make spiritual and physical preparation before anything else. Only then does anything begin" (Ortiz 1976:xiii). As yet, the whiteman's school lies beyond Pueblo prayers and songs, beyond what is "important and special to him," beyond requiring "spiritual and physical preparation," and beyond, therefore, remaining a Pueblo person. The becoming that the whiteman's school facilitates is haphazard, lacking conviction. Becoming does occur, the outside world too encompassing to bypass anyone, the Pueblo people too present in it to be passed by. The school, however, is not predictably instructive in this process. As it is, it cannot be.

---

[14]John Ogbu has written extensively about cultural discontinuity, especially in his article "Cultural Discontinuities and Schooling." Of the three types of cultural discontinuity that he identifies, "secondary discontinuities" best apply to Pueblo people—those that are "more or less enduring among castelike or subordinate minorities" (1982:291).

6

Reconstructing Memory: Imagining a Future

Santa Fe's Wheelwright Museum specializes in Indian life and culture. Occasionally, it shows a movie based on interviews with several Pueblo women potters who speak lovingly of their craft and their clay. To these talented artists, clay is not an inert substance that becomes whatever anyone wants it to be, for clay has its own dispositions, as do all "living" things.[1] One woman related her sad experience with a nearby potter who, she learned, had thrown away some clay she felt was too gritty to use. As the woman recalled this episode, she became increasingly emotional, needing to stop the interview from time to time to regain her composure. The desecration of clay deeply disturbed her; treating it as inanimate was cruel. She recovered the discarded clay and used it in her own work.

"Remember," says a Pueblo elder, "the Indian way of life is totally different from the dominant society." By so remembering, Pueblos sustain this belief, no matter that it's no longer true. Their claim of feeling "totally different" is not bombast but straightforward assertion: this, at best, is the way we've been, the way we think we are, the way we mean to be. By so believing, Pueblo people sustain hope that their ideal of who they are and must be can fortify their endeavors to remain, with integrity, a people culturally apart.

Holding to their cultural ideals in the face of an inarguably "dominant society" is an unballyhooed triumph of faith, as if to say, "Though threatened, we will not be overwhelmed. Proudly, we persist, we survive, we remain Pueblo people." To Pueblo people, ideals are facts of consequence, not fluttery dreams borne aloft by flights of revisionist history, not enticing tales told by elders on cold winter nights. Pueblo ideals function as the ground of memory but also as

---

[1]See Babcock's discussion of master potter Helen Cordero (Cochiti Pueblo), and her reference to clay as a "living substance" (1986:318).

ongoing guideposts for shaping Pueblo lives, however distant their lives may be from tribal ideals at any given time: "It isn't that Pueblo life is ideal or perfect or always the same," a Pueblo leader affirms. "I speak in the ideal and I think in the ideal because that is how we are taught." His observation, truly a critical fact, is a marvel of 500 years of post-Columbian remaining. No more than this fact is necessary to confirm Pueblo Indians as a distinctive American community: they are, indeed, like their fellow, non-Indian Americans; at the same time, they are most decisively different.

MATTERS OF IRONY

> It may be the incorrigible universalism of Western thought ... that obscures our perception of the truth: that the universal propensity to form particular and exclusive identities is not only a major source of division in society but also the primary support of social order. [Gray 1994:9]

Behavior labeled "universal propensity" locates it in our genetic structure and indicates that we could not do or be otherwise. Pueblo identity as "particular and exclusive" need not be set in the recesses of DNA for Pueblos to believe that their identity is the basis of a social order. As small social orders they've not become "a threatening source of division in society." Their particularity and exclusivity—the bases for *potential* divisiveness—lend weight to Gray's observations and feed the needless fears of those in this and every society who see conformity and homogenization as critical conditions for political health. As advocates of assimilative becoming, the fearful want groups like American Indians to metamorphose into cultural oneness with the dominant society and, accordingly, into availability for incorporation into the American mainstream. This is not the Pueblo ideal. Nor, at our best, is it the American ideal.

> And children in the warmth and security of [their] intimate, extended family group, with no intruding outside experience to modify the impact until they were forced to go to an alien school, learned [historically] what it meant to be a good Hopi. (Eggan 1976:143)

Nowadays, "intruding outside experiences" start early in the life of Pueblo children. For example, older siblings in school bring home experiences of outside education, as parents and others bring outside work and television brings the outside world . In the past, when attending the whiteman's school was a calculated anti-Indian cultural encounter, schools were more sharply, disturbingly "alien" places. When Eggan contrasts the intimacy of the family group with "an alien school," she understates the extent of contemporary overlap between home and school. Nonetheless, I join her in seeing the school as an alien institution,[2] an awkward fact in Pueblo life, a fact stuck like a fishbone that one can neither swallow nor spit out, the resulting discomfort mitigated by its familiarity.

Imbued with the ideal of harmony in their community life, Pueblo parents send their children to schools that promote cultural jangle. The sounds of education are not discordant within the schools themselves, and not within non-Indian institutional settings where the sounds belong. The sounds are discordant within Indian community life, where they don't belong and can't be kept out. The sounds, discrepant and incongruous, have yet to ring true with Pueblo harmonies, even if they seem familiar, like those of a long-time neighbor's noisy old dog who has hung around so long that you know him well and almost think he belongs just where he is. But when he ceaselessly snarls and growls and yaps—protection be damned—you become unconvinced he deserves to stay where he is, just as he is.

Indian High School is an Indian-run school. Its host community is the 19 Pueblo tribes, so it is they, not Anglo, Hispano, or Mexican groups, that provide direction to the school for whom to hire, what to teach, and how to instruct. Moreover, unlike Indian students at most schools, their students are the majority, so that their interests and their needs can be preeminent. While subject to New Mexican jurisdiction, Indian High School nonetheless has all the prerogatives of any school, public or private, religious or secular, to stamp its cultural preferences on those it serves. Indian High School "belongs" to its Pueblo community hosts in the way that American schools usually do, but because of self-imposed constraints, its education is thrust toward the culture of non-Indian society.[3] Accordingly, Pueblo people see schooling beyond its conventional accomplishments as a place of unintended means—becoming white, that lead to unintended outcomes—disrupted private lives and tribal communities.

---

[2]In this regard, Chadwick writes: "It is not lack of intelligence or ability that produces high dropout rates among Indian students, but rather a non-acceptance of an alien rite and of those aliens who have attempted to force them to participate in the rite" (1972:135). Wolcott, in his conclusion about Kwakiutl Indian youth, says, "It may happen ... that the school and teacher are perceived as alien, different, perhaps threatening to the traditional way of life" (1967:126). And Betty Jo Kramer quotes a Ponca Indian testifying before a Senate subcommittee. "'School is the enemy!'" he observed, and then added:

> By attempting to emancipate American Indian children from their families and tribes in order to 'educate' them, schools have become institutionalized alienation. The classroom becomes the battleground where American Indian children protect their integrity and identity by defeating the school system. [Kramer 1991:300]

[3]See Thomas and Wahrhaftig (1971) for further discussion of the issue of school–community fit.

At school, Pueblo children enact expressions of self that are at once both familiar—mainstream American adolescent behavior, and unsettling—the challenges to core Pueblo ideals. Since a young age, they have been compelled participants in school life, much as their parents are "compelled" participants in the institutions of the outside world. As a focal point for experiencing the cultural representations of non-Indian life, schools offer daily, ongoing occasions for an unfolding form of self that often is not assimilable with their Indian self. Thus Pueblo schools and communities require immature youth to somehow manage, join, make coherent what their own communities have neither accepted nor worked out as assimilable. Doing poorly in school may be a way to "resist fatal interruption" (Rosaldo 1986:133).

Students perceive Indian High School as an alien place despite the concerted efforts of its educators to create a school not just attended by Indian children, but "an *Indian* school for Indian children." How dismaying, then, that students can say, "This school tries to make us feel like white people and think like white people," and also that "As far as the non-Indian world, I am part of it because I am attending school." Schools are whiteman's places. *White* is a label of dishonor. "'Acting White,'" say Wax, Wax, and Dumont of Pine Ridge Sioux Indians, "is the most stinging epithet in their vocabulary" (1964:11).[4] It is no less noxious to Pueblo people. Indian High School, in fact, neither means to nor tries to make its students "feel like white people." Feeling white happens not because of its educators' plans or practices, and not because of its educators' failures or shortcomings. It happens, as the above student's words suggest, by the simple fact of attending a school whose origin, rationale, form, and content are extracted from the non-Indian, outside world.

By continuing to create a distinctive life, the tribes naturally raise children who will fail to be fully at home in the whiteman's schools. This socializing success contributes to a deep, nostalgic longing for almost any time past. Past times are more traditionally intact times. A Pueblo mother says that she knows her son would have preferred to live 500 years ago, and she thinks "older people feel the same way." A student regrets bygone ceremonial life: "I'm kind of mad

---

[4]On the one hand, the sense of threat from the judgment that tribal members are acting white has support from the findings of psychologists Oetting and Beauvais, whose research on the "correlates of cultural identification" show that "college and job success tend to be linked with Anglo identification" (1991:669). Data drawn from an unnamed Southwestern tribe reveal an inverse correlation: the stronger one's Indian cultural identification, the lower one's chances of "going to college," "getting the best job possible," and "being successful in your job" (1991:670). On the other, they report findings that show a positive correlation between high Indian cultural identification and school adjustment, a scale composed of six items, including "What kinds of grades do you get in school?," "I like school," and so on. The highest scores for school adjustment were from respondents who had both high Indian and Anglo cultural identification (1991:674).

about it because I wanted to be able to see everything and I wanted to be able to learn everything, to learn what we are supposed to." With these words, she captures most convincingly what the school lacks and what the *kiva* possesses: things so worthy of experiencing and remembering that one could say about them, "I wanted to be able to learn everything, to learn what we are supposed to." She is not alone in calling attention to the results of school and *kiva*. While Pueblo people see value in each, the *kiva* receives the blessings of the imperative, the *must* and *ought* of young and old learning "what we are supposed to." In matters of remaining, these are the aspirations of all communities and societies.

If it is true that Indian High School belongs to its Pueblo host community and, therefore, that the school is potentially available for them to shape into a fitting institution, what form might the school assume were it to become more fitting? (See Cajete [1994] for an extended answer to this question.)With these words—"In the best of circumstances, a school and its host community ... "—I began to write about a relationship, between school and community, and about a concept, fittingness, that has captured my attention since I conducted a study in Nigeria in 1965–1966 (Peshkin 1972). I do not complete this sentence; the qualifying "best of circumstances" defeats completing it. What circumstances are best depends on the perspective of inside viewers. Viewers, many in number and perspective, are neither always clear nor agree about what they think is best.

I see some similarity between the conditions of schooling in the then newly independent Nigeria and current Pueblo communities. With the passing of colonialism and the departure of British administrators and military, the dual-world case of the Muslims in Nigeria's Muslim-majority provinces involved people of the same tribe and religion, some of whom had moved into the modern sectors of society and others of whom had not. Still, there was a gulf between school and home and community, the one, creature of the modernizing, colonial-based culture, the other, rooted in traditional culture. To pass from elementary to secondary school, students took externally prepared examinations in English and mathematics, which gave these subjects importance over all others. But all students also studied Religious Knowledge, taught by a religious leader. They were listless, bored, and indifferent during most of the school day, coming to life only during Religious Knowledge. It was based on their religion, Islam, and taught in their language, Kanuri. (Otherwise, English was the language of instruction.) Though not taught by superior teachers or legitimated by the external examination, Religious Knowledge energized students because its subject matter drew upon the core of their life. If it would not promote job prospects it would inform them about the world they knew, experienced, and understood, because Islam and Kanuri define their world. In obvious and profound ways, the school, more than not being an integral part of the tribal community, in fact stood counter to its language, values, and knowledge. Accordingly, Islamic Nigeria experienced the tangled, paradoxical issues of cultural loss and gain, of conflicted remaining and becoming, but their experience was different from that of Pueblo people in at least one major respect: the immediate outside world, the one beyond traditional Kanuri communities, was dominated by people of the same religion and tribe, and so the bridging of old and new, inside and outside, was eased. In Muslim Nigeria, local educational and political officials aspired to obtain the material fruits of modernity and to retain the substance of tradition in religion and social relationships.

Closer to home, our nation's nonpublic fundamentalist Christian schools are another example of the school–host community relationship (Peshkin 1986). As private schools, they freely infuse religious doctrine as criteria, context, and content into every imaginable aspect of school life. As church and congregation desire, all employees are born-again Christians. More than this, all instructional materials are doctrinally safe and all religious aspects have priority over secular aspects, the latter clearly present because the school means also to serve the narrower ends of personal well-being in the unavoidable secular segments of their lives. The dual-world lives of students and parents place them squarely within the dominant American society. In large measure, they are culturally like other Americans, but they are taught and warned by church and school to be in this mainstream world no more than is necessary, and to avoid becoming part of it. This admonition follows Scriptural endorsement of believers staying true to their Christian path while operating in a world full of secular humanists and other enemies of the faith. In fundamentalist Christian schools, the host community's religious preferences absolutely prevail; at the same time, the school remains an American school, useful for accomplishment in American society. With secular and sacred compatibly joined in a single institution, and preeminence accorded to the sacred, the complexities of dual-world living are lessened but never fully eliminated. Complexities persist because the devotion and faith of young and old fundamentalists are challenged by the worldly attractions they must renounce but that remain ever-present, ever-alluring to them.

Although Indian High School serves children from emphatically religious communities, by tribal intent it limits its curriculum to elements of Indian history, literature, and the arts, and to Pueblo values of respect and cooperation. On principle, it excludes the religious and linguistic core of Pueblo life. On principle, therefore, the school and its host community cannot learn whether the school would be a less alien place if it was permeated by the core of Pueblo life. What exists at school of Pueblo culture assures students that they are neither denigrated nor forgotten in the pageant of learning. This is of consequence, but it does not suffice to alter the school's non-Indian character. "That is where the outside world comes in: you need the money." Thereby is the school defined.

What is missing emerged in a discussion I had with a Pueblo adult
powerful draw of the Pueblo community.

T.: "The culture is there and there's somebody calling on your innate senses
that tells you you've got to stay."

A.P.: "Is there some kind of knowledge dependency that you have on your
culture?"

T.: "Yes. That's a good way of putting it—to make you a full-fledged citizen
of your village. It is just the fact that you're not really completely whole
if you leave."

I do not pursue this matter of becoming whole. It relates to cultural practice
beyond the scope of what I can explore. I understand enough, I think, to
conclude that, as schooling is conceived and as becoming whole is defined,
success in becoming whole is not and cannot be enhanced by the current school
experience. To the contrary, becoming whole could be promoted in the Nigerian
school, in some Islamic form, at least once per day, as it could in the fundamentalist Christian school, in some Christian sense, all day, every day. The tribal
host community of Indian High School has not asked its school to be either an
integral aspect of the Pueblo "solidarity of life" (Highwater 1981:61) or "a
structure of meaning" (Marris 1974:4) that would seriously enlighten its
students about the nonschool life they live elsewhere in geographic and cultural
terms.

When I explored students' projections about their future life choices regarding marriage, friendship, and participation, I learned about their orthodoxy; in
each instance, their answers affirmed their Pueblo identity. When I explored
students' present academic behavior, I learned about malaise, their response of
uncertainty to confusion and conflict of cultural purpose.

QUESTIONS OF POSSIBILITY

Making schooling more useful to Indian students surely involves pedagogical
issues relating to the nature and content of instruction. If, as I conclude, attaining
such usefulness is less a matter of teaching strategies than of identity, of matters
that relate to remaining and becoming, then any outsider must be restrained.
My commitment to avoiding logofixion—that range of afflictions based on the
overzealous concerns of the outside observer of a group—remains unchanged,
although I confess to skirting its edges.

Avoiding prescriptions about what Pueblo communities must do—not at all
my charge—need not preclude raising questions about what they might consider thinking about. My questions reflect the point of view I've stated in

preceding paragraphs: That students generally will not do better in school until tribal communities clarify for themselves the shape and direction of remaining and becoming, a task only they can undertake. Tribal individuals lack authority to do this, except for themselves.

I begin with two sets of questions of a general nature, before continuing with several others that relate more specifically to education. What follows is my voice of the possible, an invitation for consideration, a conceivable return on the opportunity and access I was granted. Offerings of possibility may be rejected, invitations returned. Gift horses are not invariably warmly welcomed. So be it.

My questions are drawn from the conservative outlook I observed among Pueblo people. If radical advocacy for reconstructing Pueblo life exists, I did not come across it. There are persons who affirm or reject this or that Pueblo value, the emergent role of women, forms of attachment to their community. There are factions that battle ceaselessly. I learned of no organized group or pattern of protest that sought sharp breaks with their pervasive tradition or rejected the dominant society. Drawing upon the perceptions of those I learned from, including the results of community surveys that Indian High School conducted, my questions reflect, first, community survival and, second, developing a dual-world self that devotes primary loyalty to tribe while displaying competence in the dominant society.

Writer and Holocaust survivor Elie Wiesel wrote: "At critical times, at moments of peril, no one has the right to abstain, to be prudent. When the life or death—or simply the well-being—of a community is at stake, neutrality is criminal" (1990:239). Is this such a "moment of peril" in the life of Pueblo people, marked first by the school board when I sought access to Indian High School, and affirmed thereafter when young and old Pueblo citizens lamented the decline of their native languages, dreading the loss of their traditional religion and culture? Is it a time of gravity sufficient to justify mobilizing all available resources and directing them to deliberations on remaining and becoming, and on schooling's role in these processes?

To heed a warning that invites this degree of mobilization there must be optimism that desired outcomes are attainable. Anthropologist Ralph Linton wrote that "Cultures are the most flexible of adaptive mechanisms. No need of a society will go unsatisfied for long" (1972:11). His words sustain optimism. Would it be wise to fasten on to the promise of such words, drawing needed energy and hope from them, sparing them from such challenging analysis that would sap their potential to inspire? "If dreams reflect the past [and] hope summons the future" (Weisel 1990:239), is it not contemplations of the future that must be pursued with determination and persistence?

Joseph Suina, university professor, Cochiti, and, in 1995, Lieutenant Governor of his tribe, reflected on the necessity "to make sense of both worlds." He concluded, momentously, I thought, that "There was no choice left but to compete with the white man on his terms for survival. To do that I knew I had to give up part of my life" (Suina 1985:36). Is Suina's willingness to "give up" not surrender but sound strategy, at least for him and others who see their cultural duality as an emerging amalgam of what can't be avoided and of what must not be forsaken? Can he hold on to more that he values if he gives up some of what he values?

Novelist Thomas Fall (Kiowa) wrote in *The Ordeal of Running Standing* a fine tale of the meeting and clash of Indian and Anglo cultures, and the place of schooling in this clash. Almost midway through his book, one of Fall's characters reflects Suina's thought: "He was probably more interested in Indians than any white person she had ever known except the teachers at Carlisle, yet he did not want them [Indians] to do the one thing they must do in order to survive in this world—which was to change"[5] (1970:131). To what extent is cultural survival tied to change? Glibly, survival demands change. But to survive, what elements of culture must undergo what types of change? In this passage, does Fall challenge hallowed Indian tradition? By making general, overall cultural survival a higher good than the perpetuation of any particular aspect of culture, does he thereby provide a rationale for reexamining what the label of *traditional* otherwise protects and preserves from change? Is Fall indirectly suggesting the devising of procedures and plans to identify what is traditional but, nonetheless, either interferes with, or is dispensable in the cause of, advancing the greater good of overall survival? Is it reasonable to think that such a planful procedure is feasible? That there is such a greater good?

Would such a procedure include a renewed consideration of "how to imagine themselves," as professor and Minnesota Chippewa tribesman Gerald Vizenor wrote: "wherever we go we're trying to put together a new act of survival, a new imaginative state of being, a new way to deal with things.... Yes, the cultural suicides go on in the city every day. People have been so beaten that they have no energy left to know how to imagine themselves. And they only know how to be victims" (1990:165–6).

If, as a student, I am blind to the benefit of schooling, or if I cannot figure out how to incorporate those benefits I do see into my life, can I muster persistence and energy for my school tasks? Do I not need, after Vizenor, the

---

[5]Awareness of change pervades Pueblo life. Facing it, responding to it, resounds in the discourse of Pueblo life, as we hear in the optimistic words of Zuni tribesman Edmund Ladd: "We accept change, but only on our terms, which means selective change, slow change that does not destroy our cultural fabric" (Paths of Life 1994:10).

rebirth of "a new act of survival"? If Vizenor's "cultural suicides ... only know how to be victims," is there an alternative positive identity students could master—the gift of their community's imagination—that gives no credibility to the role of victim?[6]

Given the foundation of individual student behavior in community norms and values, does a newly supportive host community need to be forged? This is not to minimize either the personal responsibility or the capability of students and parents,[7] but to acknowledge that students and parents have neither means nor warrant to create the school or the community as they are now or as they are supposed to be. Thus, if students are to be able to answer questions about their future as people of two worlds, do not their communities need to clarify what forms the answers might take?[8] For example, to the extent that acting white defines what Pueblos see as antagonistic to traditional behavior, to that extent they see an oppositional outside and inside. Though such an antagonistic we–they perception may be useful to perpetuating a Pueblo sense of community, it may also prolong an unsettled, unharmonized dualism of selves. Not-

---

[6]"Quite literally," writes anthropologist Barbara Myerhoff of the Jewish elderly associated with a community center in California, "they were taken in: the reality created by the elders' imaginative statements is not limited to their own minds and beliefs ... As a result, the real world has been brought into conformity with imagination, by means of imaginative statements" (1986: 24).

[7]I have met Pueblo parents and their adolescent children who, by any measure, were successful in school and heading toward, or already in, major American universities. These exemplars of human agency clearly demonstrate what individuals can do. Moreover, they had not abandoned their commitment to Pueblo life and tradition. What some people can do does not establish firm guidelines or reassuring hope for what most ordinary people will do.

[8]A 1991 task force, co-chaired by William G. Demmert Jr. (Tlingit-Sioux) and Terrel H. Bell (then United States Secretary of Education), pursued issues relating to what was called "Indian Nations at Risk." It made many recommendations. Several recommendations, designated for "tribal governments and native communities," speak directly to the necessity for action beyond families and schools:

> Promote tribal/community responsibility and accountability for the education of all students.... Establish tribal/community education plans that define the purposes of education and outline the goals and strategies necessary to carry out those purposes. [Indian Nations at Risk Task Force 1991:25]

I would have been more encouraged by the prospects of this report if its subtitle were not "An *Educational*," but, rather, "A *Community* Strategy for Action," hewing more closely to the implications of Elaine Salinas's (Minnesota Chippewa) words: "As a community, we have allowed schools to perform at their very minimum, and this must change" (Indian Nations at Risk Task Force 1991: 17). And also to the words of Leonard Haskie (Navajo): "The children are a gift to us all, to their families, to their Indian nations, to the United States and to the world.... What is lacking in us that we cannot nurture the richness of these children?" (Indian Nations at Risk Task Force 1991:14).

withstanding the communal necessity, if not utility, of some oppositional perception, is there opportunity in defining dual-world identity issues as within the purview of both sacred and secular leadership? Would there be value in exploring the concept of harmony for its implications for locating the school within an extended embrace of what the community considers sacred?

Furthermore, continuing the point of community involvement, is a major challenge of the Pueblos the very complex task of halting the historic inverse relationship, that is, a tendency by which when one succeeds in school and the outside world, one fails in the Indian world? By some newly defined way, can students learn to think not of either this world or that world, but of both worlds? Could they learn to justly serve themselves, their families, and their communities, a feat of performance that would implicate both worlds? Could such accomplishment then foster role modeling of a host of adults who would convey with their lives what now is merely dreamt of for their children? Eventually there could be a vivid procession of such adult lives so that students never need wonder what it means when they read or hear that it is their duty to make fulfilling life choices or to walk ably in two worlds.

Is there a basis for optimism about finding solutions in what anthropologist Edward Spicer called "a type of tradition combination which results in totally new forms being accepted into a culture in such a way that they enhance the existing organization of that culture" (1961:530)? Can this be interpreted to mean that the community ought to create "new forms" of schooling? And could new forms of schooling, freshly invigorated with Indian life, resemble the old form but follow Rabbi Abraham Isaac Kook's inspiring idea that the "old must be made new, the new must be made holy" (cited in Gordis 1955:16)? Does Rabbi Kook's progression of things from old to new to holy point to establishing a spiritual foundation in schools, so that what occurs there would be not just useful but essential to master? Would a school so sanctified no longer be an alien school?

Implementing Rabbi Kook's notion is exceptionally challenging and provocative. The whiteman's school, even an Indianized one, promotes ambiguity to an extent that diminishes student motivation for pursuing success. Is there merit, then, (let alone feasibility) in fostering a school that invests its teachers with the aura of respected Pueblo elders, and its subject matter with the stuff that makes for being whole? In short, can school success be reconceptualized as tribal duty, and therefore as critical as traditional forms of participation are to tribal well being? Anthropologist Barbara Tedlock has no formula for bringing about such a reconceptualization, but while considering the "gap between the present and the disappearing past," she observes that the Zuni "are indeed dancing as they always have been, in order to bring rain and fertility, but they are also dancing the modern world into place: giving it meaning, order, perhaps even a sacred existence" (1992:141). Can a fitting school for Pueblo children be put into place by dancing, their group's prayer of movement that most prototypically embodies serious religious activity?[9] If, for reconstruction, the pedagogical particulars of schooling require serious tribal discussion, perhaps the results of such discussion necessitates legitimation by dancing, drumming, singing, fasting, and all that ritual performance entails.

Neurologist Oliver Sacks' recent work explored the rare cases of people who lived a life of near or total blindness until miraculously and suddenly they acquired sight. If sight is simply a function of the eyes, then they should recognize objects visually that previously they had known only from language and touch. If sight is not simply a matter of the eyes seeing objects, if it is, rather, the mindful matter of having learned over time how to see, then sight acquired after a lifetime without it would involve complicated challenges of perception. Sacks writes about a once-blind man who worked as a masseur and managed to live, as many people do, without sight.

> When we open our eyes each morning, it is upon a world that we have spent a lifetime learning to see. We are not given the world: we make our world through incessant experience, categorization, memory, reconnection.... When Virgil opened his eyes, after being blind for forty-five years ... there were no visual memories to support a perception, there was no world of experience and meaning awaiting him. [1993:61]

In short, the objects before Virgil's newly sighted eyes did not strike him individually or collectively as meaningful, in relationship, bearing implications. To be sure, some things were there. This he knew. But what they lacked precluded him from acting appropriately and sensibly in regard to them.

Could it be true that as experience is to visual perception, so it also is to institutional perception, and that what students need in order to see importance in schooling is, as Sacks writes, the antecedents of a "world of experience and

---

[9]Tedlock is not alone in this conception. Schechner writes, after Victor Turner, that "it is by imagining—by playing and performing—that new actualities are brought into existence" (1986: 363). And Myerhoff clarifies that such activity is not like Burke's "dancing an attitude," which Myerhoff takes to be an example of a definitional ceremony that asserts and reasserts meaning but changes nothing. She writes of dancing on behalf of assertion, redefinition, and change (1986: 268). And she writes more generally about ritual, in terms that reinforce my intent here:

> rituals always are rhetorical and didactic, inducing certain attitudes and convictions, blending wish and actuality until history and accident assume the shape of human intention. [Myerhoff 1992:131]

meaning awaiting" them?[10] Students do take eagerly to the social and athletic aspects of school life, those almost unfailingly comfortable, culturally simpler activities seen and appreciated for the good things they are. But in the absence of relevant experience, that is, of supportive memory, could it be that classroom activity, indeed, the whole academic encounter, is blurry? Its meaning and value are sensed but unfocused, possibly known slightly by bumping into, but its substance unassimilated and unmanaged because not clearly informed by past and present ideals, norms, and behavior regarding self and community.

CULTURE BOUND

Indian students attend schools of the outside world, and, in one way or another, are bound for the whiteman's culture from which the schools originated. Just where they will end up in this world cannot be predicted: the experience of schooling entails direction, but resists revealing destination. Schooling also involves the dread possibility of an unsettling, if not destructive, bound away from one's sacred tribal culture. In the twining of concerns for personal opportunity and community survival, Pueblo people are challenged to adapt and adopt, adjust and accommodate, within shifting, unfolding cultural boundaries.

Unlike the case of academically high-achieving African American students whose fellow students accuse them of "acting white" (Fordham and Ogbu 1986), Pueblo students may evoke this observation from Pueblo adults who do not mean to belittle academic success but who fear, resist, and worry about school-learned behavior that is not culturally Pueblo-bound. In the African American and the Pueblo cases—alike in some respects but basically different—a traditional social order is being denied by behavior that someone interprets as contrary to the good of this order. In the former, it is the social order as conceived by peers; adults are not prone to make the accusation. In the latter, it is the social order as conceived by tribal community; peers are not necessarily similarly threatened. In both cases, school success antagonizes because others see it as contrary, oppositional behavior.

Paradoxically, modest school success may make it easier to stay in place, to think it is agreeable to do so, and to avoid conjuring up alternatives that would

---

[10]Bissinger cites Stephen Bogaerts, a teacher at Proviso West High School in Illinois, in regard to the reactions of students to the importance of schooling: "Schools are about hope and the future.... But if you don't have hope and you don't believe in the future, schools are oddly anachronistic. That's why students are not intimidated by failure. If they fail, it's too bad. Failure is the same as success" (Bissinger 1994:50). Seeing "hope and the future" may be relevant to the antecedents of a "world of experience."

unsettle tradition. As now imagined and constituted for Pueblo students, schooling may offer as much opportunity as they have learned to wish for, as much success as they can manage to take advantage of. If they possessed higher levels of aspiration, would they then be agents of accelerated social change, with its accompanying challenges and tensions? In short, are they doing well enough by an implicit set of standards that differs from those that educators and others endorse? Would it be subversive if they generally did better? Is how they are doing congruent with some prevailing but unspoken code, so that what appears as rule breaking—that is, not doing well in school—really is role conformity,[11] consistent with the norms of another, implicit conception of the student role?

How finally ironic to think that the Pueblo student malaise I have identified may be functional, at least in the short run, for their traditional culture. It is not the malaise of students who consciously, conspiratorially aspire to modest achievement, knowing that if they do they exalt tradition and its perpetuation. It is the malaise of sensed cultural disharmony, often of clear awareness of ambiguity, by students who simultaneously know and do not know the worth of education, and who, as they acknowledge, struggle to live acceptably in two worlds: one grounded in memory ever more gilded, a fantasy ideal of misty eyes but also of meaning; the other grounded in opportunity tarnished by uncertainty, aversiveness, and threat. Memory favors each world unequally.

Finally, the ambiguity of Pueblo lives rests on another fact: though they live in two worlds, they have but one soul. Their hearts, their deepest longings, their source of being and identity rest most securely in the comfort and ideals of Pueblo communities. This triumph, a celebratory accomplishment, puts perversity in its place (albeit, not to rest). Thereby are they also bound.

---

[11]Ordinarily, but never completely, students inherit their school roles from their peers and predecessors. Models of how to be a student surround them from the outset of their school days. If there is not a single right model, there are a few dominant acceptable ones. Thus, the model of malaise reproduces itself. Circumventing the clutch of this learned model is possible—not rare, but uncommon. While occasionally annoyed by its outcomes, students mostly carry on as if they believe that what they do enjoys the stamp of normalcy.

Epilogue

... the hope for gain is shadowed everywhere by the fear of loss.

—*Clifford Geertz, 1995*

I

Having written a prologue, I was obliged by a sense of symmetry to write an epilogue. Having explored the association between academic underachievement and the issues of identity, remaining and becoming, and cultural survival, I also felt that I had some reflective recapitulation that wanted expression. Thus I close with these thoughts almost 5 years after I began my year of living at Indian High School.

I write this book with a keen sense of having wended my way through a mass of observations and thoughts, some I feel obliged to stay clear of, others I think I ought to include. The ultimate shape of my text, now at last forthrightly before me, makes clear that I do not plan to add my outlook to that pall of authorial predecessors who, despairing of Indian people, see their tomorrows cast in the mold of eternally hopeless yesterdays. There are indeed such books to write; their underlying facts would, at times, often poke through to my consciousness.

I make a choice; a choice, somehow, is thrust upon me. More than feeling charged to contribute something positive by those who reminded me at the outset of why I was permitted to conduct the study, I realize, even more strongly in retrospect, that the several score student essays I read, the numerous interviews I conducted, and the year-round ritual, feast-day dances, talk, and meal offerings I was party to were, in sum, celebrations of Pueblo past, present, and future; they were testimonials, affirmations of sorts, both large and small, to fete, promise, and prospect. They were not, as I'd heard older Pueblo men boast in my hearing, conspiratorial amusements of the type they concoct for the benefit of camera-clad tourists. I believe what I was told, the researcher's conceit, perhaps, but my essential rationale for feeling reassured that I was present as a professional, not as a tour-bus passerby.

II

Researchers are never innocent, however much they presume otherwise. To say that I meant to relate to the persons I interviewed and observed as a data-collecting learner is never to suggest that I was just a sponge, soaking up information, devoid of will and expectation. I was, of course, the non-Indian outsider, a member of an inquiring, acquisitive profession, who makes a living not primarily by collecting data, but by formulating and writing about what I have learned. I am the avowed subjective learner, purpose in hand, with passion aplenty, and I resided in Pueblo life as both collector and writer. Thus, I run the risk of doing damage in two respects.

With my fieldworker-collector role behind me, whatever damage I may have done is done. In the interest of minimizing damage in my role as inscriber, I invited reactions to my manuscript from Indian High School's Pueblo superintendent and school board and from several teachers and members of various Pueblo tribes. School officials did not reply. I interpret their silence to mean indifference or that they think what I wrote will do no harm. Pueblo teachers assure me that I got things reasonably straight, as they see them, and that I have not dealt inappropriately with tabooed matters. Other Pueblo members were similarly reassuring, although some expressed discomfort at even my infrequent reference to the sacred *kiva*. Past and present educators were most affirming by their observation that my "explanation" of the too-familiar phenomenon of limited academic success usefully clarified why their best instructional efforts so often were futile. Others thought I should have developed more emphatically the point of Pueblo community responsibility for the integration of schooling with Pueblo life, daring, I surmise, to place the obligation for this integration on community leaders, rather than on educators.

Neither the officials' silence (whatever it may mean) nor the affirmation is necessarily generalizable to other tribal members, who may have other views and stakes in school and community. Moreover, I do assume that my many questions in chapter 6 point to alternative futures. Questions by their very nature invite someone's reconsideration, and if I assume the need for reconsideration, then surely I must see something amiss. Shades of logofixion: no innocence here!

III

Although I no longer listen regularly to National Native News, my attention remains drawn to things Indian wherever they appear—in the media, on bookstore shelves, or with personal associations. I have withdrawn from the daily contact that for several years kept me fully focused on Pueblo life in general and on its issues of school and community in particular.

At this distance in time and place from New Mexico, I can reflect on the Pueblo case within the context of several decades spent exploring the school–community relationship. Clearly, in relatively homogeneous sociocultural circumstances, such as the rural and fundamentalist Christian settings of my past research, a good fit between school and home culture is relatively easy to establish and maintain. The prerogatives of local control and the historical responsiveness of American schools to their host communities can combine to create schools that reflect the values and behaviors of home and community reasonably well.

Yet even where such a good cultural fit prevails, the matters of remaining and becoming are imbued with tension and controversy, for school and community exist within contexts of change, and change requires modifying the nature of the fit. These modifications hold implications for a school's curriculum and instruction, but seldom, as in the Pueblo case, for questioning the essential thrust of the school, and, therefore, for exploring accommodations that go straight to the heart of the institution. At its heart, we ask basic questions about a school: Whose life does it serve? Whose life should it serve? Is it the life of the school's clients—its community, families, and children? How is the host community affected by what the school may be required to do that accommodates nonlocal community values and behavior? These are the matters of becoming that derive from the larger society. Such fundamental considerations take laypersons and professionals alike beyond the usual borders of their deliberation, and thus beyond where their thinking and discourse usually prepares them to go.

By their own acknowledgment, Pueblos young and old frame their lives within a concern for survival, turning to the whiteman's world, for schools that are linked to economic development, and turning to their Indian world, for the *kiva* and other communal institutions that sustain tradition. But schools are not just about economic agency, and tribal socialization is not just about Pueblo tradition. Given all that both worlds entail, the school-community relationship is flawed, fundamentally incoherent and incongruent—a fit, in short, that does not work. As schools now stand, any one that Pueblo children would attend is, for self and community, disruptive.

IV

From the moment I heard Pueblo persons refer to the "outside world," my attention was aroused. I had frequented such a place. During the several years of my fundamentalist Christian project (Peshkin 1986), I lived in a setting that fully deserved the designation of "outside world." To call some place the "outside world" is to dismiss it as *not me, not mine, not us, not my people.* It is to say that for me it is a place of less acceptance, comfort, and security, as well as a place less known to me and less understanding of me. There are few to no consequences if I say this about the Amish, a small, isolated religious group who live down the road from me in Illinois. If I say this about fundamentalist Christians, I dramatically change the consequences: The Amish do not aspire to transform my life; the fundamentalist Christians do—my life and my world, in ways at odds with almost everything I value.

Should they choose to do so, Pueblo Indians could speak similarly. They could say that in their outside world they seldom reveal their Indian names, and they never discuss their religion. While they do not walk there quite as strangers, still they may look strange to others, and they often feel estranged. Their identity as American is of the hyphenated-minority type; by look and life they unwittingly challenge others to accept them. For their differences, their otherness, they may be sometimes denigrated and demeaned, sometimes glorified and romanticized: a discordant note in the symphony of popular national imagination, which lumps them stereotypically with all Indian people—in tipis, dancing and costumed, with scalps and raids, speaking monosyllabically, or whooping on horseback. Their history, seen skewed from the outside by outsiders, is a partial telling of a partialled life.

V

When I think about schools and their impact on Pueblo communities, I envision peeling away. To begin with, I see Pueblo communities in their ideal sense as cultural wholes, a convivial human ball that is integrated, compact, and cohesive. And then I see schools operating like pincers that inexorably pick away at children in an effort to remove them from their cultural whole. Sometimes the removal is total. More often it is incomplete, and the children are variably attached to their Indian world, sometimes loosely or tightly, and sometimes at numerous points in between. Pueblo people are similarly, if usually more loosely, attached to the non-Indian world. Consequently, the Pueblo cultural whole becomes a riot of partial attachments, while its members strive to live within it in some ideal sense. They are conscious of the loss that comes with partiality, concerned to reconnect and overcome the peeling effects, and never sure how this can be accomplished.

Coincident with this image is one related to activity within the ball itself, inchoate and incipient activity, a confusion of intentions whose antecedents may be agreed upon but whose future may not. This is an image less of peeled and peeling individuals nicely returning to place than of individuals colliding in search of a reconstituted whole. They are attuned to the fact that something is missing and thus that something is needed, but they are unsure and disagree about just how to proceed.

Together these images convey a picture of opposing inward and outward activity, on the one hand, and of unaccomplished synthetic activity, on the other. The dialectic is ongoing and disturbing, not so much an encounter of wills as of forces sometimes mistaken for but still struggling to become will.

A third image, to return to my themes, depicts remaining and becoming as contending forces or engaged warriors. On one side are Pueblo Indians, the conscious combatants, knowingly present in an arena of confrontation, and often aware of the high stakes: nothing less than identity, or who a person or a group will turn out to be. On the other side are non-Indians, the impersonal giants of change; although no longer driven by an overtly assimilating official policy, they nonetheless occupy the arena. If they do not intentionally drive Pueblos away from tradition, they do so anyway simply by the arrogance of their mass and momentum.

The two forces are unbalanced and asymmetrical in every respect. As for the stakes, the outside world will carry on much as it always has, while the Pueblo world literally has everything to gain or lose. As regards the weapons at its disposal, the outside world grows ever more powerful as the scale of its institutional means grows ever larger. Thus the contest is markedly uneven.

VI

Gertrude Stein's poetic dismissal of Oakland, California, as a place that, when reached, a visitor found no *there* there, is denigration with a vengeance. She might have believed the same about Pueblo communities had she ever seen them to comment on them; this is clearly not so for their tribal members. Though far from flawless, Pueblo communities succeed as places of powerful memory—as conflicted memory, to be sure, but definitely as places with an incomparable there for Pueblo people. For where else can they learn and perpetuate who they are and who they can become but in *kivas* and homes and plazas and mountains cathected beyond the understanding of most outsiders, and beyond the capability of most communities anywhere. Pueblo memory favors the distant past, the repository of tribal glory and esteem, the certain, accessible source of meaning and belonging. Pueblo communities enclose the there of one's past, present, and future, the there of one's life and culture. Confounded by conflict and angst, Pueblo memory nonetheless stands preeminent. It is where tribal members are both trapped and transformed.

Perhaps most basic to my perspective is the distinction that "Places of Memory" connotes: school and the whiteman's world, *kiva* and the Pueblo world. Together they fully embody all of where Pueblo people live. At this time in their history, their several places of memory cannot be distinguished simply by necessity (the non-Indian world), and by choice (the Indian world). Wherever Pueblo people live, both necessity and choice prevail; the two aspects fuse, blend, and mix, now favoring one place, then the other. But, as I have said, all that I have learned points triumphally to *kiva* and Pueblo as the essential place of memory.

Indeed, I now think of the Pueblo's inside and outside worlds as even more sharply and distinctively framing their identity, a result of seeing Pierre Nora's clarification of memory and history. In Nora's terms, school and society are part of history; *kiva* and Pueblo are part of memory. History, he clarifies, "attaches itself to events," whereas "memory attaches itself to sites" (1989:22). In this sense, events somewhat have the character of removed happenings, the stuff of elsewhere. Sites, to the contrary, contain events within a continuity of structures—the institutions of community. The dailiness and ordinariness of these event-embodying structures sustain memory.[1]

Nora's excellent essay elaborates this history-memory duality: "memory is life ... history is reconstruction"; "memory ... [ties] us to the eternal present ... and history is a representation of the past"; "memory installs representation within the sacred ... and history ... releases it again"; and "memory is blind to all but the group it binds ... history belongs to everyone" (1989:8–9).

These distinctions of the particular and the universal, the local and the cosmopolitan, evoke the novelty of what Pueblo youth are invited to understand and live with when they enter their outside world.

VII

For Pueblo children, the school experience is seldom unbearable, certainly not a surprise—it has been around too long for that. But as an unassimilated good, it lies anomalously over community life, its potential for jobs and money inviting, on the one hand, but bearing unwelcome prospects, on the other—of cultural disruption, racism, and rejection. At home, students can feel they

---

[1]For an excellent elaboration of the processes involved in collective memory, see Paul Connerton's *How Societies Remember* (1989).

measure up; away, they feel they suffer by comparison. Basically unsure how to walk the confluence of Indian and non-Indian worlds, students are timid; they flounder, and too often fail to live comfortably as citizens of either world.

Their school lives abound with *buts*, the anticipatory utterance of doubt, reservation, uncertainty: I could work harder, but … ; I should work harder, but … ; I could have gone to college, but….; I should have stayed in college, but …; I didn't want to have children so young, but …; School is OK, I like school, but …. Schooling and its promises skid along the surfaces of tribal life, acknowledged but not anointed, lacking roots to anchor students in networks of appropriate cultural meaning.

What conditions of school and community would be necessary for a school serving Pueblo children to foster both individual and communal well-being? Many types of nonpublic schools provide suggestive models; none of them seem to me quite suitable for the Pueblo theocracies. It is daunting to think of reconstructing school and community, so that what Pueblo people often now experience as the painfully confounded choice of either this world or that, they would come to perceive as desirably complementary worlds. Undertaking such reconstruction is exacerbated by the unending press of normal events that challenge us to live from day-to-day with Monday's problems, Tuesday's joys, ad infinitum.

I do not know in what particulars of change can be found the "resolution" of Pueblo duality and its consequences for school success. I assume, however, that the task of imagining these particulars can be located nowhere else but in the joint endeavors of sacred and secular Pueblo leadership to shape a future. Resolutions, by their nature, insist on the certainty of a future.

VIII

In this final point, I reflect on what I have written in this epilogue. Its relatively cheerless mood derives from my sense of the Pueblos' underlying concern for their cultural survival, and of the modest contribution of Indian High School to this survival. Survival, one of two aspects of Pueblo life, is too serious to ignore, slight, or underplay. The other is the aspect more of the moment, where laughter, joy, and accomplishment are plentiful. It is an unlimited moment of friends and family, of met obligations and accomplishment, where the pleasures of form and sound, aroma and color, those in nature and those of human creation, prevail. Thinking essentially about survival, I wrote an epilogue that slighted this latter aspect. At best, writing illuminates, clarifies, dramatizes, and reveals. At best, I concede, writing also distorts and conceals.

References

Aldrich, Hope. 1991. Keepers of the treasures. *Santa Fe Reporter*, 20–26 Nov. 6.

Allen, Paula Gunn. 1983. *The woman who owned the shadows*. San Francisco: Spinsters Ink.

Asante, Molefi Kete. 1993. Racism, consciousness, and Afrocentrism. In *Lure and loathing*, ed. Gerald Early. New York: Penguin Press.

Au, Kathryn H. 1980. Participant structures in a reading lesson with Hawaiian children. Analysis of a culturally appropriate instructional event. *Anthropology and Education Quarterly*, 11(2): 91–115.

Au, Kathryn H., and Cathie Jordan. 1981. Teaching reading to Hawaiian children: Finding a culturally appropriate solution. In *Culture in the bilingual classroom: Studies in classroom ethnography*, eds. Henry H. Trueba, Grace Pung Guthrie, and Kathryn H. Au. Rowley, MA: Newberry House.

Babcock, Barbara. 1986. Modeled selves: Helen Cordero's 'Little People.' In *The anthropology of experience*, eds. Victor W. Turner and Edward H. Bruner. Urbana, IL: University of Illinois Press.

Basso, Keith. 1979. *Portraits of "the Whiteman."* Cambridge: Cambridge University Press.

Ball, Jane A. 1990. Alliance or schism: The complexity of Pueblo culture. In *Culture and the anthropological tradition*, ed. Robert H. Winthrop. Lanham: University Press of America.

Barringer, Felicity. 1990. Pueblo parents feel generation gap. *New York Times Education*, 24 Oct., B-9.

Bennett, John. 1946. The interpretations of Pueblo culture: A question of values. *Southwestern Journal of Anthropology*, 2(4):361–374.

Bentley, Lis. 1995. Relentless. *Pasatiempo,* August 18–24:60–61.

Berry, John W. 1980. Acculturation as varieties of adaptation. In *Acculturation: Theory, models, and some findings*, ed. Amado M. Padilla. Boulder, CO: Westview Press.

Bissinger, H. G. 1994. We're all racist now. *New York Times Magazine*, 29 May, 26–33, 43, 50, 53–54.

Blanchard, Evelyn Lance. 1983. The growth and development of American Indian and Alaskan native children. In *The psychosocial development of minority group children*, ed. Gloria Johnson Powell. New York: Brunner/Mazel Publishers.

Bodine, John J. 1972. Acculturation processes and population dynamics. In *New perspectives on the Pueblos*, ed. Alfonso Ortiz. Albuquerque: University of New Mexico Press.

Bruner, Edward M. 1953. Assimilation among Fort Berthold Indians. *The American Indian*, 6:21–29.

——. 1956. Primary group experience and the process of acculturation. *American Anthropologist*, 58(4):605–623.

——. 1961. Mandan. In *Perspectives in American Indian cultural change*, ed. Edward Spicer. Chicago: University of Chicago Press.

——. 1986. Ethnography as narrative. In *The anthropology of experience,* eds. Victor W. Turner and Edward M. Bruner. Urbana, IL: University of Illinois Press.

Bureau of the Census. 1992. *1990 Census of population, New Mexico.* Washington, DC: Department of Commerce.

Cajete, Gregory. 1994. *Look to the mountain: An ecology of indigenous education.* Durango, CO: Kivaki Press.

Carter, Stephen L. 1993. The black table, the empty seat, and the tie. In *Lure and loathing,* ed. Gerald Early. New York: Penguin Press.

Cary, Lorene. 1991. *Black ice.* New York: Knopf.

Chadwick, Bruce A. 1972. The inedible feast. In *Native Americans today: Sociological perspectives,* eds. Howard Bahr, Bruce Chadwick, and Robert Day. New York: Harper & Row.

Chin, Frank. 1991. *Donald duk.* Minneapolis: Coffee House Press.

Clifton, James A. 1989. *Being and becoming Indian.* Chicago: Dorsey Press.

Cobos, Rubén. 1983. A *dictionary of New Mexico and Southern Colorado Spanish.* Santa Fe: Museum of New Mexico Press.

Coles, Robert. 1977. Eskimos, Chicanos, Indians. Vol. IV of *Children of crisis.* Boston: Little, Brown and Company.

Collier, John, Jr. 1988. Survival at Rough Rock: A historical overview of Rough Rock demonstration school. *Anthropology and Education Quarterly,* 19(3):253–269.

Coltelli, Laura. 1990. *Winged words: American Indian writers speak.* Lincoln: University of Nebraska Press.

Cone, Kathy. 1994. Crying in the mostly urban wilderness. *New York Times Book Review,* 8 Aug., 24–25.

Connerton, Paul. 1989. *How societies remember.* Cambridge: Cambridge University Press.

deBuys, William. 1995. *Review of Beyond the four corners of the world,* by Emily Benedek. *New York Times Book Review,* 22 October, 39.

Dehyle, Donna. 1991. Empowerment and cultural conflict: Navajo parents and the schooling of their children. *Qualitative Studies in Education,* 4(4):277–297.

——. 1992. Constructing failure and maintaining cultural identity: Navajo and Ute school leavers. *Journal of American Indian Education,* 31(2):24–47.

Deloria, Vine, Jr. 1991. Higher education and self determination. *Winds of Change,* Winter, 19–25.

DeVos, George A., and Marcelo M. Suárez-Orozco. 1990. *Status inequality: The self in culture.* Newbury Park, CA: Sage.

Dorris, Michael. 1989. *The broken cord: A family's ongoing battle with fetal alcohol syndrome.* New York: Harper & Row.

Dozier, Edward P. 1956. The value and moral concepts of Rio Grande Pueblo Indians. In *Encyclopedia of morals,* ed. Vergilius Ferm. New York: Philosophical Library.

——. 1964. The Pueblo Indians of the Southwest. *Current Anthropology* 5(2):79–97.

——. 1983. The *Pueblo Indians of North America.* Prospect Heights, IL: Waveland Press.

DuBois, W. E. B. 1969. *The souls of black folk.* 2nd ed. New York: New American Library.

Early, Gerald. 1993. *Lure and loathing: Essays on race, identity, and the ambivalence of assimilation.* New York: Penguin.

Eggan, Dorothy. 1976. Instruction and affect in Hopi cultural continuity. In *Schooling in the cultural context,* eds. Joan I. Roberts and Sherrie K. Akinsanya. New York: David McKay.

Emerson, Gloria J. 1995. Of Indian language and art. *The Magazine,* 2 August, 20.

Erickson, Frederick. 1984. School literacy, reasoning, and civility: An anthropologist's perspective. *Review of Educational Research,* 54(4):525–546.

———. 1993. Transformations and school success: The politics and culture of educational achievement. In *Minority education: Anthropological perspectives*, eds. Evelyn Jacob and Cathie Jordan, Norwood, NJ: Ablex.

Fall, Thomas. 1970. *The ordeal of running standing*. New York: McCall Publishing Co.

Fergusson, Erna. 1931. *Dancing gods: Indian ceremonials in New Mexico and Arizona*. Albuquerque: University of New Mexico Press.

Ferraro, Thomas J. 1993. *Ethnic passages*. Chicago: University of Chicago Press.

Foehr, Stephen. 1994. *Body and soul*. Chicago Tribune, 3 May, 15.

Foley, Douglas. 1991. Reconsidering anthropological explanations of school failure. *Anthropology and Education Quarterly*, 22:1, 60–86.

Fordham, Signithia, and John Ogbu. 1986. Black students' school success: Coping with the burden of 'acting white.' *The Urban Review*, 18:3, 176–206.

Fox, Robin. 1973. *Enounter with Anthropology*. New York: Harcourt, Brace, Jovanovich.

Fuchs, Estelle, and Havighurst, Robert J. 1972. *To live on this earth: American Indian education*. Garden City, NY: Anchor Books.

Fynn, Arthur J. 1907. *The American Indian as a product of environment with special reference to the Pueblos*. Boston: Little, Brown.

Geertz, Clifford. 1995. *After the fact: Two countries, four decades, one anthropologist*. Cambridge, MA: Harvard University Press.

Goldfrank, Esther. 1952. The different patterns of Blackfoot and Pueblo adaptation to white authority. In *Acculturation in the Americas*, Vol II. ed. Sol Tax. Chicago: University of Chicago Press.

Gordis, Robert. 1955. *Judaism for the modern age*. New York: Farrar, Straus, & Cudahy.

Gray, John. 1994. Why things fall apart. Review of *The problems of order* by Dennis H. Wrong. *New York Times Book Review*, 13 Feb., 9.

Grobsmith, Elizabeth S. 1981. *Lakota of the Rosebud: A contemporary ethnography*. New York: Holt, Rinehart & Winston.

Gutiérrez, Ramón A. 1991. *When Jesus came, the Corn Mothers went away*. Stanford: Stanford University Press.

Harrod, Howard L. 1995. *Becoming and remaining a people: Native American religions on the Northern Plains*. Tucson: University of Arizona Press.

Hawley, Florence. 1937. Pueblo social organization as a lead to Pueblo history. *American Anthropologist*, 39(3):504–522.

Heath, Shirley Brice. 1983. *Ways with words*. New York: Cambridge University Press.

Heilman, Samuel C. 1977. Inner and outer identities: Sociological ambivalence among orthodox Jews. *Jewish Social Studies*, 39:227–240.

Henze, Rosemary C., and Lauren Vanett. 1993. To walk in two worlds—or more? Challenging a common metaphor of native education. *Anthropology and Education Quarterly*, 24(2):116–134.

Highwater, Jamake. 1981. *The primal mind: Vision and reality in Indian America*. New York: Harper & Row.

Hobson, Geary, ed. 1979. *The remembered earth*. Albuquerque: University of New Mexico Press.

Hoffman, Eva. 1989. *Lost in translation: A life in a new language*. New York: Penguin Books.

Horgan, Paul. 1970. *The heroic triad: Essays in the social energies of three southwestern cultures*. New York: Holt, Rinehart & Winston.

Horse, Perry G. 1994. Inaugural address. *Artwinds*, Summer, 8.

Indian Nations at Risk Task Force. 1991. *Indian Nations at risk: An educational strategy for action*. Washington, DC: U.S. Department of Education.

Indians push sovereignty issue. 1993. *New Mexican*, 26 April, 1–2.

"Indians work to save a language and their heritage." 1992. *Education Week*, 20 May, 1.

Indyke, Dottie. 1994. Coyote explores the active art of listening. *Pasatiempo*, 23 June, 18, 50.

Jacob, Evelyn, and Cathie Jordan (eds.). 1993. *Minority education: Anthropological perspectives.* Norwood, NJ: Ablex.

Jen, Gish. 1991. *Typical American.* Boston: Houghton Mifflin.

Joe, Jennie R. 1994. Revaluing Native-American Concepts of Development and Education. In *Cross-cultural roots of minority child development,* eds. Patricia Greenfield and Rodney R. Cocking. Hillsdale, NJ: Lawrence Erlbaum Associates.

John-Steiner, Vera P., and Osterreich, H. 1975. *Learning styles among Pueblo children: Final report to National Institute of Education.* Albuquerque: University of New Mexico Press.

Jones, Donna. 1991. The best of both worlds. *Albuquerque Journal*, 22 Feb., 16.

Jordan, Cathie. 1984. Cultural compatability and the education of ethnic minority children. *Educational Research Quarterly*, 8(4):59–71.

———. 1985. Translating Culture. *Anthropology and Education Quarterly,* 16(2):105–123.

Kane, Cheikh Hamidou. 1972. *Ambiguous adventure.* London: Heinemann.

Kaufman, Dorothy. 1994. Tuba City Primary School Program focuses on Navajo culture and language. *Forum, 17*(3), 1, 4.

Kessell, John L. 1979. *Kiva, cross, and crown.* Washington, DC: U.S.Department of Interior.

Kincaid, James. 1992. Who gets to tell their stories? *New York Times Book Review*, 3 May, 1, 24–29.

King, A. Richard. 1967. *The school at Mopass: A problem of identity.* New York: Holt, Rinehart & Winston.

Klass, Perri. 1992. Tackling problems we thought we solved. *New York Times Magazine,* 13 Dec., 54–58, 61–62.

Knox, Martha. 1993. Their mother's keepers. *Sierra*, March–April, 51–57, 81–84.

Kramer, Betty Jo. 1991. Education and American Indians: The experience of the Ute Indian Tribe. In *Minority status and schooling*, eds. Margaret A. Gibson and John U. Ogbu. New York: Garland Publishing, Inc.

Kress, Stephen. 1993. One of the few. *Crosswinds,* 5:9.

Kugelmass, Jack (ed.). 1988. *Between two worlds: Ethnographic essays on American Jewry.* Ithaca: Cornell University Press.

LaFromboise, Teresa D., and Delores Subia Bigfoot. 1988. Cultural and cognitive considerations in the prevention of Indian adolescent suicide. *Journal of Adolescence*, 11:139–153.

LaFromboise, Teresa D., Hardin L. K. Coleman, and Jennifer Gerton. 1993. Psychological impact of biculturalism: Evidence and theory. *Psychological Bulletin, 114*(3):395–412.

Levine, Donald N. 1985. *The flight from ambiguity: Essays in social and cultural theory.* Chicago: University of Chicago Press.

Linton, Ralph. 1972. The distinctive aspects of acculturation. In *The emergent Native Americans: A reader in culture contacts*, ed. Deward Walker, Jr. Boston: Little, Brown & Co.

Little Soldier, Lee. 1985. To soar with eagles: Enculturation and acculturation of Indian children. *Childhood Education*, 61(3):185–191.

Lopate, Philip. 1991. Review of *Black ice* by Lorene Cary. An epistle from St. Paul's. *New York Times Book Review*, 31 March, 7.

Ludeman, W. W. 1960. The Indian Student in College. *Journal of Educational Sociology*, 33:333–336.

Luftig, Richard L. 1983. Effects of schooling on the self-concept of Native American students. *The School Counselor*, 30(4):251–260.

Lurie, Theodore. 1991. Shattering the myth of the vanishing American. *Ford Foundation Letter*, Winter 22(3): 1–5.

Malouf, David. 1993. *Remembering Babylon.* New York: Vintage Books.

Marris, Peter. 1974. *Loss and change*. London: Routledge & Kegan Paul.

McDermott, Ray P. 1974. Achieving school failure: An anthropological approach to illiteracy and social stratification. In *Education and cultural process: Toward an anthropology of education*, ed. George D. Spindler. New York: Holt, Rinehart & Winston.

————. 1987. The explanation of minority school failure again. *Anthropology and Education Quarterly*, 18:361–364.

McDermott, Ray P. and Kenneth Gospodinoff. 1979. Social contexts for ethnic borders and school failure. In *Nonverbal behavior*, ed. Aaron Wolfgang. New York: Academic Press.

McKnight, Reginald. 1993. Confessions of a wannabe Negro. In *Lure and loathing*, ed. Gerald Early. New York: Penguin Press.

McLaughlin, Daniel. 1992. *When literacy empowers: Navajo language in print*. Albuquerque: University of New Mexico Press.

Mehan, Hugh. 1991. *Sociological foundations supporting the study of cultural diversity*. Washington, DC: Center for Applied Linguistics.

Mehan, Hugh, Lea Hubbard, and Irene Villanueva. 1994. Forming academic identities: Accommodation without assimilation among involuntary minorities. *Anthropology and Education Quarterly*, 25:2, 91–117.

Merton, Robert K., and Elinor Barber. 1963. Sociological ambivalence. In *Sociological theory, values, and sociocultural change*, ed. Edward A. Tiryakian. New York: Free Press of Glencoe.

Moyers, Robert. 1941. *A history of education in New Mexico*. Ph.D. diss., George Peabody College for Teachers.

Mura, David. 1991. *Turning Japanese: Memoirs of a Sansei*. New York: Atlantic Monthly Press.

Myerhoff, Barbara. 1986. "Life not death in Venice": Its second life. In *The anthropology of experience*, eds. Victor W. Turner and Edward M. Bruner. Urbana, IL: University of Illinois Press.

————. 1992. We don't wrap herring in a printed page: Fusion, fictions, and continuity in secular ritual. In *Remembered lives*, ed. Marc Kaminsky. Ann Arbor: University of Michigan Press.

New traditions from New Mexico. 1991. *USA Weekend*, 9–11 August, 12.

Nora, Pierre. 1989. Between memory and history: Leslieux de mémoire. *Representations*, 26:7–25.

O'Brien, Eileen. N.d. *Native American education*. Part 1, 16. N.p.

Oehlsen, Nadia. 1992. Chief fights today's Cherokee enemies: Illiteracy, racism. *News Gazette*, 25 October, 3.

Oetting, E. R., and Fred Beauvais. 1990–1991. Orthogonal cultural identification: The cultural identification of minority adolescents. *International Journal of Addictions, 25*(5A and 6A):655–685.

Ogbu, John. 1978. *Minority education and caste: The American system in cross-cultural perspective*. Orlando, FL: Academic Press.

————. 1982. Cultural discontinuities and schooling. *Anthropology and Education Quarterly*, 13(4):290–307.

————. 1986. Caste stratification as a risk factor for mental retardation in the United States. In *Risk and intellectual and psychological development*, eds. Dale C. Farran and James D. McKinney. Orlando: Academic Press, Inc.

————. 1987. Variability in minority responses to schooling: Nonimmigrants vs. immigrants. In *Interpretive ethnography of education: At home and abroad*, eds. George and Louise Spindler. Hillsdale, NJ: Lawrence Erlbaum Associates.

————. 1991. Immigrant and involuntary minorities in comparative perspective. In *Minority status and schooling: A comparative study of immigrant and involuntary minorities*, eds. Margaret A. Gibson and John U Ogbu. New York: Garland Publishing, Inc.

——. 1992. A cultural–ecological approach to the study of minority education: A framework. *Fireside Chat* presented at the annual meeting of the American Educational Research Association, San Francisco.

Ogbu, John U. and Maria Matute-Bianchi. 1986. Understanding sociocultural factors: Knowledge, identity, and school adjustment. In *Beyond language: Social and cultural factors in schooling language minority youngsters*, ed. California State Department of Education. Sacramento, CA: California State University–Los Angeles, Evaluation, Dissemination, and Assessment Center.

Ortiz, Alfonso. 1969. *The Tewa World: Space, time, and becoming in a Pueblo society*. Chicago: University of Chicago Press.

——. 1994. The dynamics of Pueblo cultural survival. In *North American Indian anthropology: Essays of society and culture*, eds. Raymond J. DeMallie and Alfonso Ortiz. Norman: University of Oklahoma.

Ortiz, Simon. 1975. Survival this way. In *Carriers of the dream wheel: Contemporary Native American poetry*, ed. Duane Niatum. New York: Harper & Row.

——. 1976. *Going for the rain*. New York: Harper & Row.

——. 1987. The language we know. In *I tell you now*, eds. Brian Swann and Arnold Krupat. Lincoln, NB: University of Nebraska Press.

Parsons, Elsie Clews. 1939. *Pueblo Indian religion*. Vol. 2. Chicago: University of Chicago Press.

Paths of Life. 1994. *Arizona Alumnus*, 9–10.

Peshkin, Alan. 1972. *Kanuri schoolchildren: Education and social mobilization in Nigeria*. New York: Holt Rinehart & Winston, Inc.

——. 1982. *The imperfect union: School consolidation and community conflict*. Chicago: University of Chicago Press.

——. 1986. *God's choice: The total world of a fundamentalist Christian school*. Chicago: University of Chicago Press.

——. 1988. In search of subjectivity: One's own. *Educational Researcher, 17*(7):17–22.

——. 1991. *The color of strangers, the color of friends: The play of ethnicity in school and community*. Chicago: University of Chicago Press.

——. 1994. *Growing up American: Schooling and the survival of community*. Prospect Heights, IL: Waveland Press.

——. 1995. The complex world of an embedded institution: Schools and their constituent publics. In *School–community connections*, eds. Leo Rigsby, Maynard Reynolds, and Margaret Wang. San Francisco: Jossey Bass.

Philips, Susan U. 1983. *The invisible culture: Communication in classroom and community on the Warm Springs Indian Reservation*. New York: Longmans.

Polgar, Steven. 1960. Biculturation of Mesquakie teenage boys. *American Anthropologist, 60*(2):217–235.

"Pueblo leaders say water settlements may be acceptable." 1992. *New Mexican*, 23 April, A4.

Restak, Richard. 1992. Review of *A chorus of stones* by Susan Griffin. *New York Times Book Review*, 15 Nov., 15.

Reyhner, Jon. 1992. American Indian cultures and school success. *Journal of American Indian Education*, 32:1, 30–39.

Rodriguez, Richard. 1982. *Hunger of memory: The education of Richard Rodriguez, an autobiography*. Boston: D. R. Godine.

Rodríguez, Sylvia. 1994. Subaltern historiography on the Rio Grande: On Gutiérrez's *When Jesus Came, the Corn Mothers Went Away*. *American Ethnologist*, 21(4): 892–899.

Romero, Mary E. 1992. *Identifying giftedness among Pueblo Indians*. Report to the Office of Educational Research and Improvement. New Mexico.

Rosaldo, Renato. 1986. Ilongot hunting as story and experience. In *The anthropology of experience,* eds. Victor W. Turner and Edward M. Bruner. Urbana, IL: University of Illinois Press.

Rose, Wendy. 1983. Neon scars. In *I tell you now*, eds. Brian Swann and Arnold Krupat. Lincoln, NE: University of Nebraska Press.

Rotheram-Borus, Mary. 1993. Biculturalism among adolescents. In *Ethnic identity*, eds. Martha E. Bernel and George P. Knight. Albany: SUNY Press.

Sacks, Oliver. 1993. To see and not to see. *New Yorker,* 10 May, 59–73.

Sampson, Edward E. 1985. The decentralization of identity. *American Psychologist*, 40(11):1203–1211.

Sando, Joe. 1992. *Pueblo nations.* Santa Fe, NM: Clear Light Publishers.

Schechner, Richard. 1986. Magnitudes of performance. In *The anthropology of experience*, eds. Victor W. Turner and Edward M. Bruner. Urbana, IL: University of Illinois Press.

Scheper-Hughes, Nancy. 1987. The best of two worlds, the worst of two worlds: Reflections on culture and field work among the rural Irish and Pueblo Indians. *Comparative Study of Society and History*, 29(1):56–75.

Seals, David. 1991. *Powwow highway:* Author comments. *Winds of Change,* Winter, 6–7.

Seigel, Bernard. 1952. Suggested factors of culture change at Taos Pueblo. In *Acculturation in the Americas*, ed. Sol Tax. Chicago: University of Chicago Press.

Smith, Anne M. 1966. *New Mexico Indians: Economic, educational and social problems.* Santa Fe: Museum of New Mexico.

Smith, Watson. 1990. *When is a kiva? And other questions about Southwestern archeology.* Tucson: University of Arizona Press.

Spicer, Edward H. 1961. Types of contact and processes of change. In *Perspectives in American Indian culture change*, ed. Edward H. Spicer. Chicago: University of Chicago Press.

———. 1962. *Cycles of conquest: The impact of Spain, Mexico, and the United States on the Indians of the Southwest, 1533–1960.* Tucson: University of Arizona Press.

———. 1972. Social structure and the acculturation process. In *The emergent Native Americans*, ed. Deward E. Walker, Jr. Boston: Little, Brown & Company.

Spindler, George, and Louise Spindler. 1971. *Dreamers without power: The Menomini Indians.* New York: Holt, Rinehart & Winston.

Steiner, Stan. 1968. *The new Indians.* New York: Harper & Row.

Stevens, Anthony. 1991. Excerpt from *On Jung,* quoted in *New York Times Book Review*, 43.

Stocking, Kathleen. 1990. *Letters from the Leelanau: Essays of people and place.* Ann Arbor: University of Michigan Press.

Suárez-Orozco, Marcelo M. 1990. Migration and education: United States-Europe comparisons. In *Status inequality: The self in culture*, eds. George De Vos and Marcelo M. Suárez-Orozco. Newbury Park, CA: Sage.

Suina, Joseph H. 1985. And then I went to school. *New Mexico Journal of Reading*, 5(2):34–36.

———. 1991. There's nothing sinister in Pueblos' secretive ways. *Albuquerque Tribune,* 28 June, 18.

———. and Laura B. Smolkin. 1994. From natal culture to school culture to dominant society culture: Supporting transitions for Pueblo Indian students. In *Cross-cultural roots of minority child development*, eds. Patricia Greenfield and Rodney R. Cocking. Hillsdale, NJ: Lawrence Erlbaum Associates.

Tedlock, Barbara. 1992. *The beautiful and the dangerous: Dialogues with Zuni Indians.* New York: Penguin Books.

Tharp, Roland G. 1994. Intergroup differences among Native Americans in socialization and child cognition. In *Cross-cultural roots for minority child development,* eds. Patricia Greenfield and Rodney R. Cocking. Hillsdale, NJ: Lawrence Erlbaum Associates.

——. and Ronald Gallimore. 1988. *Rousing minds to life: Teaching, learning and schooling in social context.* Cambridge, U.K.: Cambridge University Press.

Thomas, Robert K. and Albert L. Wahrhaftig. 1971. Indians, hillbillies, and the education problem. In *Anthropological perspectives on education*, eds. Murray L. Wax, Stanley Diamond, and Fred O. Gearing. New York: Basic Books.

Trimble, Joseph E. 1977. The sojourner in American Indian community: Methodological issues and concerns. *Journal of Social Issues,* 33(4):159–174.

Trueba, Henry T. 1991. Comments on Foley's Reconsidering anthropological explanations. *Anthropology and Education Quarterly,* 22:1, 87–94.

Ugna-Oju, Dympna. 1993. Hers: Pursuit of happiness. *New York Times Magazine,* 14 Nov., 40, 42.

Villani, John. 1992. Hama-Ha aims to put focus back into storytelling tradition. *Pasatiempo,* 13 March, 32.

Vizenor, Gerald. 1990. Gerald Vizenor. In *Winged words: American Indian writers speak,* ed. Laura Coltelli. Lincoln, NB: University of Nebraska Press.

——. 1994. *Manifest manners. Postindian warriors of survivance.* Hanover, N.H.: Wesleyan University Press.

Vogt, Lynn A. Cathie Jordan, and Roland G. Tharp. 1987. Explaining school failure, producing school success: Two cases, *Anthropology and Education Quarterly,* 18(4): 276–286.

Walker, Deward, Jr., ed. 1972. *The emergent Native Americans: A reader in culture contacts.* Boston: Little, Brown & Co.

Waters, Frank. 1970. *The man who killed the deer.* 2nd ed. New York: Washington Square Books.

Wax, Rosalie H. 1971. *Doing fieldwork: Warnings and advice.* Chicago: University of Chicago Press.

Wax, Murray L., Rosalie H. Wax, and Robert V. Dumont. 1964. *Formal education in an American Indian community.* Society for the Study of Social Problems Monograph no. 1. Atlanta: Emory University.

Weisel, Elie. 1990. *From the kingdom of memory: Reminiscences.* New York: Summit Books.

White, Leslie A. 1935 The Pueblo of Santo Domingo, New Mexico. *Memoirs of the American Anthropological Association,* 43.

——. 1942. The Pueblo of Santa Ana, New Mexico. *American Anthropologist,* 44(4):3–360, pt. 2.

——. 1962. The Pueblo of Zia, New Mexico. *Bulletin of the Bureau of American Ethnology,* no. 184. Washington, DC: U.S. Government Printing Office.

Wolcott, Harry F. 1967. *A Kwakiutl village and school.* New York: Holt, Rinehart & Winston.

Author Index

Subject Index